MR. JEFFERSON'S RIVER

THE RIVANNA

Minnie Lee McGehee
William E. Trout, III

THE FLUVANNA COUNTY HISTORICAL SOCIETY • PALMYRA, VIRGINIA

Mr. Jefferson's River: The Rivanna
Minnie Lee McGehee and William E. Trout, III

Copyright © 2001 by The Fluvanna County Historical Society

Published by The Fluvanna County Historical Society, P.O. Box 8, Palmyra, VA 22963.
Additional distribution by The Van Doren Company, 100 Carlton Road, Suite 2,
Charlottesville, VA 22902. 434-973-2201; fax 434-973-8964; email vandoren@cstone.net.

ISBN 0-9713605-0-2

Library of Congress Control Number: 2001095594

Cover Photograph: Upriver at Crofton, by Betty McGehee

EDITORIAL PRODUCTION: THE VAN DOREN COMPANY
COVER DESIGN: WILLIAM VAN DOREN
TEXT DESIGN: WILLIAM VAN DOREN WITH MINNIE LEE MCGEHEE
COPY EDITING: THE VAN DOREN COMPANY AND SAYRE GRAVES

Printed in Korea

2 4 6 8 10 9 7 5 3 1

CONTENTS

FOREWORD 1

INTRODUCTION 3

1. THOMAS JEFFERSON'S RIVER 11

2. THE RIVANNA COMPANY:
   WING-DAM BUILDING FOR BATTEAUX, 1806–1827 19

3. THOMAS JEFFERSON AND THE RIVANNA COMPANY 23

4. THE RIVANNA NAVIGATION COMPANY:
   LOCKS AND DAMS FOR BATTEAUX, 1827–1850 27

5. LOCKS AND DAMS FOR HORSE-DRAWN BOATS, 1850–1854 37

6. NAVIGATION NUMBERS 63

7. THE RIVANNA'S VILLAGES 69

8. VANISHING TOWPATHS: GOOD-BYE TO AN ERA 87

9. VESTIGES: MEMORIES AND DISCOVERIES 91

10. THE FUTURE OF AN AMERICAN TREASURE 99

NOTES 101

INDEX 106

ABOUT THE AUTHORS 108

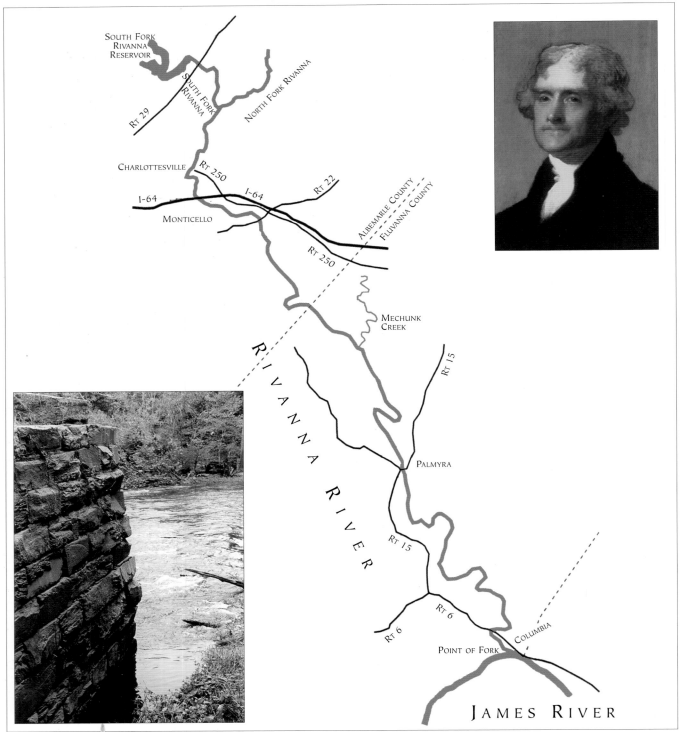

SOUTH FORK
RIVANNA
RESERVOIR

SOUTH FORK RIVANNA

NORTH FORK RIVANNA

RT 29

CHARLOTTESVILLE

RT 250

I-64

I-64

RT 22

MONTICELLO

RT 250

ALBEMARLE COUNTY

FLUVANNA COUNTY

MECHUNK
CREEK

RT 15

RIVANNA RIVER

PALMYRA

RT 15

RT 6

RT 6

COLUMBIA

POINT OF FORK

JAMES RIVER

PHOTOGRAPH OF THE PALMYRA LOCK AND DAM BY CHARLES M. WINKLER; MAP ADAPTED BY PERMISSION FROM *VIRGINIA WILDLIFE*, APRIL 1993.

FOREWORD

This book is the history of an era in Albemarle and Fluvanna counties when boats and mills on the Rivanna River provided a means of transportation and industry in this section of Piedmont Virginia. There were four different eras of transportation on the Rivanna: dugout canoes (both single and double), batteaux aided by wing dams, then batteaux in deeper water made possible by dams and narrow locks built during the first half of the nineteenth century, and, beginning in the early 1850s, horse-drawn canal boats—the first mode of river transport not dependent on human power—which required higher dams, larger stone locks and a towpath.

From 1763 until c. 1915, the Rivanna made the agricultural economy possible and profitable. Then the navigation system and its boats yielded to the railroads, and soon the water-powered mills also disappeared.

The years of the Rivanna navigation were unique and were fondly remembered—a time before interstate highways, fast automobiles and mammoth trucks fashioned a new age.

* * * * *

An earnest attempt has been made to include credit to those who gave us Rivanna-related pictures or who took special photographs for us during the last 35 years. If we have failed, it was not due to a lack of gratitude. For the most part, those taken by us, the authors, are published without a specific credit. Copies of all in our collections will now be deposited in the archives of the Old Stone Jail Museum in Palmyra, maintained by the Fluvanna Historical Society.

Editors do not agree on the correct spelling of the type of boat called the Virginia Batteau. Members of the Virginia Canals and Navigations Society have done exhaustive research on the name and chose the historic spelling "batteau," instead of "bateau," for their publications. In loyalty to the members of that Society, who have worked hard to study and preserve the Rivanna and other waterways of Old Virginia, we use the spelling they prefer.

Many of the sites described in this work can be seen from the river, but most of them are in private ownership and permission must be gained to explore in depth.

* * * * *

We wish to express our gratitude to the Elizabeth Ireland Graves Foundation, Sayre Graves and William Winston, whose generosity made this publication possible. We thank Robert Lum, P.L.S. for the maps included. We thank the Albemarle County Historical Society and the staff of their library; the Fluvanna Historical Society, especially the successive presidents Mike Gillespie and Marvin Moss; and our friends Ellen Miyagawa, Nancy Dunnavant and David Bearr for all their work and loyal encouragement. Also, we are indebted to each member of the McGehee family who shared our interests, and who assisted us in this research and composition, each step of the way.

Minnie Lee McGehee
William E. Trout, III

"Mountains distant & near, smooth & shaggy, single & in ridges, a little river hiding itself among the hills so as to show in lagoons only, cultivated grounds under the eye and two small villages."

INTRODUCTION

If a river can belong to one man, the little Rivanna, snaking across the Virginia Piedmont, flying a pennant of sycamore and birch, is assuredly Thomas Jefferson's.
— *Mike W. Edwards*

Mankind always has been fascinated by running water. The early English settlers in Virginia clung to the banks of the rivers, which were vital as a means of transportation to market, and to power mills. Thomas Jefferson's river was the Rivanna. He studied the possibilities of the Rivanna River, the biggest tributary of the James above the fall line.

The river was named early in Virginia's history, according to the custom of naming streams for royalty. The name honored Queen Anne, as did the eventual county name, Fluvanna. The Rivanna was also often called the North Fork (of the James), as the James west of Columbia and the mouth of the Rivanna was first named the Fluvanna River.

Thomas Jefferson's life began and ended on the highlands above the Rivanna River, and, though his duties and travels took him to places far removed from Virginia's Piedmont, his land along the Rivanna was always home. From the lawn of his beloved Monticello, his "little mountain," the terrain falls steeply to the Rivanna, the conical tulip poplars marching down to meet their reflections in the stream. The Scotch-broom that he planted on his mountaintop has migrated from its original plantation and now trails its greenery in the Rivanna's cool currents.

No one has measured the contributions a river can make in a boy's development, as he roams the banks, explores the shallows and depths, wades and swims, his keen young eyes and inquisitive mind registering all the wonders and myster-

VIRGINIA CREEPER.

ies of the riverine world. When as a young man Jefferson took his first canoe ride to inspect the Rivanna as a passage for boats, did he envision the raindrops from his hatbrim flowing into the waters of the Atlantic, or did he dream of representing his wilderness country in the courts of Europe?

Documented history shows that, during his lifetime, with his mills and his vision of river commerce, Thomas Jefferson shaped the Rivanna for his lifetime and ours. As a young man, before he became President of the United States, Jefferson made a record of his philanthropic accomplishments, and he placed first on the list his efforts to make the Rivanna River navigable—the Declaration of Independence was second!

It may well be that his boyhood home on the Rivanna shaped the life of Jefferson, starting him on his road to greatness. Certainly, when he first ran for public office, his greatest claim on the allegiance of his constituency was his successful campaign to open the Rivanna for navigation. He won a seat in the Virginia Assembly at the tender age of 26 because voters, especially those in southeast Albemarle (later Fluvanna County), appreciated this public service.

To the west of Monticello, Jefferson could feast his eyes on the hazy tree-covered slopes of the Blue Ridge Mountains as they stretched away to meet the blue of the sky. On the eastern ridges of this blue elevation, the Rivanna has its beginning, and in the shady hollows it is continually reborn as the cool, clear water from springs and rivulets begins a long journey to the sea.

For the most part, the Rivanna's headwaters are all in Albemarle County, although it does steal some water from Greene County in small streams, including Preddy Creek. The highland rills become creeks, such as Stockton and Dollins, which make their singing courses down the mountains to form Mechums and Moormans rivers, and they in turn join Buck Mountain Creek and become the South Fork of the Rivanna River. According to some maps the North Fork springs into being bearing its full name, and is joined from the north by Preddy Creek and from the east by the waters from the slopes of the Southwest Mountains. By this time the two branches have a respectable flow and merge to form the eastern boundary of the city of Charlottesville.

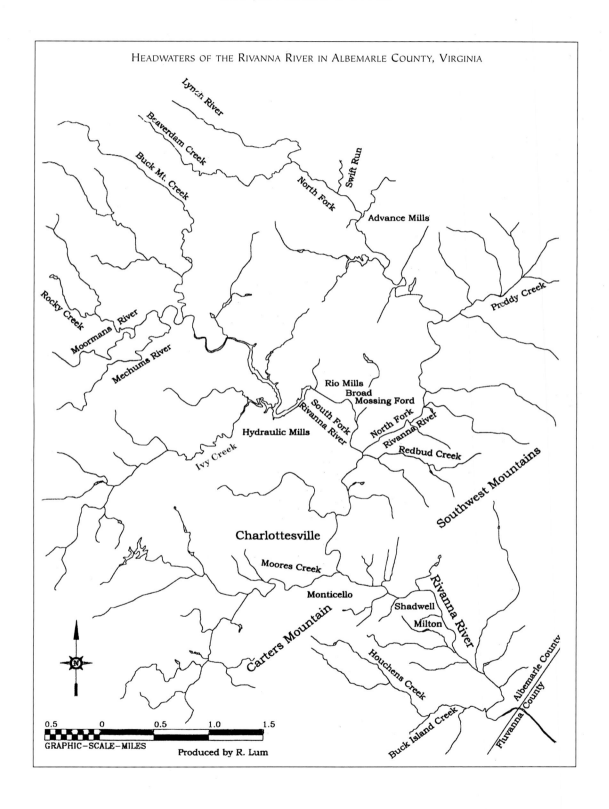

HEADWATERS OF THE RIVANNA RIVER IN ALBEMARLE COUNTY, VIRGINIA

Lynch River

Beaverdam Creek

Buck Mt. Creek

Swift Run

North Fork

Advance Mills

Rocky Creek

Preddy Creek

Moormans River

Mechums River

Rio Mills
Broad
Mossing Ford

South Fork
Rivanna River

North Fork
Rivanna River

Hydraulic Mills

Redbud Creek

Ivy Creek

Southwest Mountains

Charlottesville

Moores Creek

Monticello

Shadwell

Milton

Rivanna River

Carters Mountain

Houchens Creek

Albemarle County

Buck Island Creek

Fluvanna County

0.5   0   0.5   1.0   1.5

GRAPHIC—SCALE—MILES

Produced by R. Lum

5

GREAT BLUE HERON IN THE RIVER.

From the heights of his mountain, Jefferson could trace the valley of the Rivanna from the north of Charlottesville far down into Fluvanna. Looking eastward he could watch the fog rise from the meandering stream in the lowlands, a vista he is said to have described as his "sea view." In the other direction he could watch the summer storm clouds roll over the Blue Ridge, storms he called the "work house of nature." But he was a landholder, as well as a naturalist, and knew that the same storms that replenished the Rivanna also brought floods to threaten his mills and his cropland.

The strong civic leaders who followed Mr. Jefferson carried forward and expanded his dream of successful navigation on the Rivanna. As the years passed, they improved the waterway to be more typical of the boat passages of Europe. Beginning the year after Jefferson's death, the navigation structures were rebuilt for better passage of batteaux, and soon the citizens of Albemarle and Fluvanna began to plan a further extension of his vision for the Rivanna: a towpath and horse-drawn canal boats.

In today's world we can explore Thomas Jefferson's river for ourselves, launching our canoe at the foot of Monticello on the outskirts of Charlottesville near the mouth of Moore's Creek. We follow a southeast course, twisting and turning our way to the Point of Fork, where the Rivanna joins the James River at the town of Columbia.

Each curve of the stream brings surprises. At times we drift in gentle pools between lush lowground fields; at other times we maneuver through white water, sluiced between boulders and cliffs of looming stone and hemlock, our ears filled with the roar of tumbling water. As we go through the Southwest Mountains, we navigate down the falls that powered Jefferson's Mills. The early batteaux did not go through these rapids; they went around them through Jefferson's millrace.

Before leaving Albemarle, we see Buck Island Creek flow in from the west, and, not far into Fluvanna, Mechunk Creek brings its water from a northeast watershed in both counties. Mechunk hits the Rivanna as the river circuits a solid rock escarpment on its west bank, a dramatic junction.

We pass the mouths of many small streams as they enter the river almost stealthily between surprisingly narrow and high banks; even the larger creeks are not easy to spy: Boston, Burke, Cunningham, Raccoon, Ballenger, Long Island, Carys, Roundabout, Dog, Gum and "Mt. Misory," names that linger in the mind—names that define our section of the Piedmont. The merging currents from the tributaries form deltas at these junctions—small islands covered with sprouting alders, sycamores, beech and river birch.

After we lose sight of the low mountains, some of the most challenging water we encounter is created by the remains of dams built to provide slack water for navigation and energy to operate grain mills. For one canoeing down this rather small but entrancing river today, it is difficult to imagine that boats large enough to carry cargo and paying passengers made their way both upstream and down, and that the water powered great turbines, gears and grinding stones.

In our time a water-powered mill is only a rare curiosity found on an afternoon's scenic drive. Yet, if we were to float the river and take the time to go ashore, the remains of the mills, dams and navigation locks are there to be seen along the Rivanna. This river transport and these mills (many of them operating in Jefferson's lifetime) were once the lifeblood of our Piedmont counties.

The massive stone locks of the Rivanna navigation were beautifully built and were intended to last for many generations. Today their remains make the Rivanna's the best-preserved and most complete navigation in the state. There is something romantic about a ruin, juxtaposing, as it does the relentless forward motion of human history and the cyclical timelessness of nature. For those who love the Rivanna, these ruins are endlessly fascinating.

There are many who bring their boats to the river to fish for smallmouth bass, catfish, bream or carp, but there are others who prefer just to float, paddling only when looming rocks make it necessary. Once our canoe is launched beneath a highway bridge, and our day on the river begins, we enter a different world, a world ever so quiet and seemingly untouched by human hands. Lulled by the moving water, by the never-ending flow, we are enticed by vistas that beckon and unfold, enclosed by banks lined with green trees and cascading Virginia Creeper or high walls of stone

BETTY McGEHEE

CARDINAL FLOWER.

7

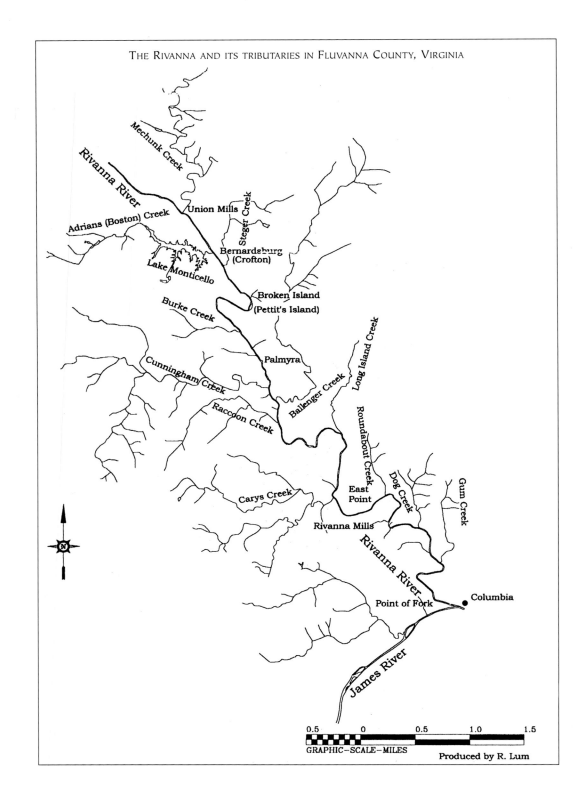

THE RIVANNA AND ITS TRIBUTARIES IN FLUVANNA COUNTY, VIRGINIA

GRAPHIC–SCALE–MILES

Produced by R. Lum

and lichen, rocky crags that rise in Paleozoic humps against the sky.

With changing agricultural practices, the lowground fields are now covered with pasture grasses or timber and no longer make the Rivanna run muddy; only occasional earth-moving construction mars its beauty. Leaning over the stern of our boat to peer into the clear water, we watch the fish fin their way upstream; we find mussel shells that vary so much in shape, color and size they could have escaped from a nursery rhyme, and we study the sandy bottom in search of other treasures only a river can bestow.

Soon a wonderful sandy island invites us to picnic and explore, swim and splash about, and lie in the sun. On the river, far removed from the harrying bustle of modern life, the stillness broken only by the ripple of the water, we are free to watch a blue heron prinking his way along the shallows, to meet a distracted wood duck protecting her young, to admire wildflowers on the banks, and to enjoy the bright colors of garden phlox and day lilies deposited by floods. We find our-selves mesmerized by the ever-flowing, unending movement of water—water, the essence of life itself.

A RIVANNA HEMLOCK CLIFF. *Typical rock formation on our stream. The river's course is northwest to southeast, and, for the most part, the rock strata slant downward from northeast to southwest.*

He who hears the rippling rivers in these degenerate days will not utterly despair.
—Henry David Thoreau

"... I see that the petition of Ashlin to build a dam across the river adjacent to Ross's lands, & consequently not far above its mouth has been reported reasonable. [W]here a mill dam assists navigation it is well to allow it because it becomes a public good. McGruder's I believe stands on this ground. Wood's I am assured does not, and is a great obstruction to the speed necessary with us to take advantage of accidental tides [freshets]."

Th: Jefferson

(1809)

1

THOMAS JEFFERSON'S RIVER

Thomas Jefferson began the first organized effort to improve the Rivanna River for navigation in 1763. His interest in using the Rivanna as an avenue for shipments of farm produce began when he returned home to Shadwell upon completing his education. He was successful in making the Rivanna navigable for canoes and double canoes, and his efforts were rewarded when he first ran for public office. He won the seat in the General Assembly held by Dr. Thomas Walker of Castle Hill, a giant of his time and Jefferson's mentor.

Later Jefferson wrote:

> *The Rivanna River had never been used for navigation, scarcely an empty canoe had ever passed down it. Soon after I came of age I examined it's [sic] obstructions, set on foot a subscription for removing them. got an act of assembly past [passed] & the thing effected, so as to be used completely & fully for carrying down all our produce.*

Jefferson offered more details in another letter:

> *In 1763 (I was then not quite of age) learning that a canoe, with a family in it, had passed and repassed several times between Buck island creek in Albemarle and the*

Byrd Creek in Goochland, and that there were no serious obstacles between [here and] Adam's falls (now Magruder's) I went in a canoe from Mountain falls [Milton falls] to Adam's and found that section of the river could be made navigable for loaded boats by removing loose rock only. I set on foot a subscription and obtained £200. Dr. [Thomas] Walker our representative, got inserted in the act here cited, a nomination for 11 trustees, with authority to do what was necessary for effecting the navigation of this river, from the south upwards. Roger and George Thompson, then living on the river, undertook and Executed the work . . . .

Jefferson persuaded Walker to include the Rivanna in a navigation act before the General Assembly, and this 1765 act called for making the Rivanna navigable from its mouth up to the falls at Milton, three-fourths of a mile below Jefferson's mill. Jefferson was one of the trustees appointed for the £200 that he had raised for work on the Rivanna.

TATUM'S ESSAY ON TOBACCO (1800)

DOUBLE DUGOUT CANOE.

Later, Jefferson and his son-in-law and neighbor, Thomas Mann Randolph, spent £100 of their own funds to cut a straight 60-yard sluice through the Milton falls to extend the navigation up to Jefferson's Shadwell Mills. To Jefferson's disgust, in 1812 the navigation company blocked off his own sluice and blasted another that had a twist in it, which tended to throw descending boats against an island. He complained that this discouraged boatmen from using the sluice and wasted all his previous efforts at the Milton Falls. As a result he had to send goods down to Milton by wagons or in small boats as far as the falls, where the loads were transferred to "regular river craft" (batteaux) for the 90-mile trip from Milton to Richmond.

After the river was first improved, produce, including tobacco, wheat and flour, was sent down the Rivanna by dugout canoes such as the Indians had used. A single craft about 16 feet long could carry only two or three hogsheads of tobacco. For greater stability and capacity, two canoes were lashed together. These double canoes, each 50 or 60 feet long and four to five feet wide—an invention of the Reverend

BATTEAU REPLICA. James River Batteau Festival.

Robert Rose—could transport eight or nine heavy hogsheads down the upland streams.

When the great flood of 1771 destroyed many of the dugout canoes, Virginia's James River batteau was "invented" by Benjamin and Anthony Rucker, and (later patented) these became the "regular river craft"—the whitewater freighters. They were a unique Virginia invention that spread through the Southern states—wooden, flat-bottomed, highly maneuverable shallow-draft boats, pointed at both ends, up to seven feet wide and about 60 feet long. When the first James River batteau was launched, Jefferson was on hand to witness it.

These cargo boats were not paddled like canoes. In order to travel against the current, a batteau was fitted with a board atop the gunwales at each side. These served as walkways for men equipped with long metal-tipped poles, which they planted in the riverbed before walking the length of the craft, fore to aft. Thus, in treadmill fashion, they propelled the boat upstream past the fixed points of the poles. Going downstream, they depended on the current, guiding the batteau with a sweep (a long oar) at each end.

LOW WATER. In summer droughts, the Rivanna's water level falls drastically. In Jefferson's time, droughts meant that canoes and batteaux could not take his flour downstream to market. Today the river is the source of water for a section of Albemarle County, the city of Charlottesville, and several subdivisions along the stream. Downstream, the Rivanna must also flush the treated sewage from these communities.

The batteaux were required to be registered. In Fluvanna County in 1792 William C. Bugg registered his batteau: "Sir Please enter my bote in the offis and Send me a tickkitt... markid and Nombred No. 1 WM*C*BUGG Fluvanna Count in Cappittil letors a Cordin to law."

The new batteaux did not eliminate the use of double dugout canoes, as T. J. Wertenbaker pointed out:

> *The Rivanna proved invaluable to the American cause during the Revolution. Point of Fork, the present Columbia, was a military depot, and powder, arms, wheat and even coal were stored there . . . . Men experienced in river navigation recommended that canoes rather*

BROKEN BRIDGE AT MILTON, C. 1929. The bridges and the mills, dams and locks on the Rivanna suffered from repeated floods. At the height of the batteau era, Milton was a thriving village, larger than Charlottesville.

than batteaux be used in moving stores, since they could pass in places too shallow for heavier boats . . . .

When some powder sent up the river to the arsenal got wet, the commissary ordered that all canoes be lashed together in pairs as Rose had done, and when the post was warned that the British were coming to raid the supply depot, canoes were used to move the military stores up the James and Rivanna rivers to hide them from the enemy.

Land transport on the primitive roads of the day was slow and very costly; river navigation made it possible for Virginia's inland settlers to make a living. However, Rivanna transport was subject to the river's whims. Untold numbers of batteaux were wrecked, their cargoes lost or ruined by water; the records are full of such events, as well as accounts of drought, ice or floods, which often interrupted shipping altogether.

Jefferson was concerned about floods, and noted one on April 22, 1804, in his Garden Book:

[A] great fresh in the Rivanna this day, it was above the top of the hopper in my toll mill. by marks at Henderson's distillery in Milton it wanted 6. feet of being as high as that in 1795 which wanted but 3 f. of being as high as the great fresh on the 26th of May 1771.

In 1806 Jefferson was most optimistic and wrote that he considered the Rivanna a reliable route to market:

> *The river is regularly boatable about 7. or 8. months from the beginning of November (not obstructed by ice once in 2 years & then only a few days) and in the Summer months the boats always hold themselves in readiness to catch the accidental tides [freshets or minor floods] from showers of rain, so that a great deal is done in that season, and there is rarely any accumulation of produce for want of a tide.*

Thirteen years later, he suffered a long drought. Navigation was impossible; a hard year for Jefferson:

> *I am entirely in despair, dear Sir, on account of the obstinate state of our river. Such a thing has never been known before since the opening its navigation 50. years ago, that the drought of the summer which commenced in June should meet the ice of the winter, without a single interval for a boat to make a trip. for the 100. Bar. [Barrels] of flour I sent from here Oct. 10. I learn that 60. barrels are still lying in the lower part of the river, and none of the boats which went then have yet got back. I have flour enough ready in the mill, but see no prospect of getting it off unless a plentiful & warm rain should come to our aid, fill the river and melt and carry off the ice.*

As river transportation developed, warehouses were built along the river for the state inspection of tobacco. There planters exchanged hogsheads of tobacco for inspection and shipment to market. (Perhaps this state inspection was the first act of government to regulate agricultural produce.) In 1785 the Rivanna Warehouse, one of the earlier warehouses in Virginia, was established at Point of Fork, at the confluence of the Rivanna and James rivers. Three years later the legislature created the town of Columbia at this junction of the rivers.

Milton (at "The Shallows" of the Rivanna) was then the head of navigation, and became the shipping center for perhaps three-quarters of Albemarle County—the Port of Albemarle. Henderson's Warehouse and the town of Milton were established in the same year: 1789. Nicolas's Warehouse was built across the river from Henderson's.

POINT OF FORK. The Rivanna and James rivers meet here. It probably looked much like this when the first settlers from Jamestown found it and named both the upper James and the North Fork for Queen Anne—the Fluvanna and Rivanna, respectively. Some historians have considered this point the site of Rassawek, capital of the Monacan nation. Many Indian artifacts have been found here.

Halfway down the Rivanna, a fourth tobacco inspection warehouse was established in 1802 on the lands of Allen Bernard adjoining Bernardsburg, a town established in 1796. Records show Fluvanna folk wrote the name as they spoke it: Barnerdsburg or Barnesburg. As river navigation declined, these two towns of Milton and Bernardsburg no longer flourished. Until recent years the abandoned streets of old Milton could still be seen from the air. The remains of the buildings at Bernardsburg were destroyed when development of the Lake Monticello subdivision began in 1968.

"The navigation of the Rivanna [by canoes and batteaux], extends naturally from it's [sic] mouth at Columbia, up to where it passes thro' the South West mountains: that is to say to the Sandy falls, at the foot of the bed of the mountain. [T]hese are about 150 yards above the Shadwell mills, and a mile above the town of Milton. I say it extended <u>naturally</u>; because from the mouth up to the Milton falls, it needed a little help only . . . ."

Th: Jefferson

(1813)

2

THE RIVANNA COMPANY: WING-DAM BUILDING FOR BATTEAUX, 1806–1827

The Rivanna Company was incorporated in 1806 with the power to charge tolls, to make a profit for its subscribers, and to make improvements on the river for navigation. The company's directors in 1810 were George Divers, William H. Meriwether, Nimrod Braham, John Kelly and treasurer Dabney Minor.

The 1814 General Assembly authorized William Wood, owner of Wood's Mill on the Rivanna near Columbia, to take over the improvement and maintenance of the navigation from Milton to the James, and to charge tolls for its use. By 1817 Wood was actively engaged in straightening and deepening sluices and building wing dams at 27 falls, shoals and fords between Milton and Columbia. An 1828 survey of the Rivanna notes the location of many of these.

The wing dams were not elaborate masonry or wooden structures, but were long, low, dry-laid walls or mounds of river stones. They extended out from one or both shores to force the river water into channels, called sluices. If the sluice was near a bank, the men poling a batteau upstream could get out on the bank and use a rope to pull the boat manually through the channel, but if the sluice was in the middle of the river, it presented a problem.

UPSTREAM IN ALBEMARLE

Above Charlottesville the Rivanna was improved with sluices and wing dams as far as Hydraulic Mills, five miles up the South Fork, and to Martin's Mill (also called Barksdale's), four miles up the North Fork. In 1820 local residents cleared

COLLECTION, ALBEMARLE COUNTY HISTORICAL SOCIETY

WARREN ANDERSON

WARREN ANDERSON

WOOLEN MILLS. An aerial view of the dam from the mid-twentieth century; a more recent photo of the dam; and the smokestack of the abandoned Charlottesville-Albemarle Railway power plant, erected in 1914, which used water from the Rivanna. (The smokestack can be seen from Interstate 64 as well as from the river.) The dam, built of stone, is the only one on an original navigation site still holding back the flow of the Rivanna. It is located at the old Pireus, "the Port of Albemarle."

the North Fork for three more miles up to William Tulloch's Mill. George Martin was instructed to put a lock in his mill-dam for the use of batteaux going up to Tulloch's, but he probably never did, because in 1845 Martin stated that his mill (not Tulloch's) was at the head of navigation on the North Fork.

The several milldams on the Rivanna were required by law to have navigation locks for batteaux. The company's report in 1818 lists seven wooden locks: three at Shadwell (Jefferson's Mills) and one each at Campbell's (Buck Island), Union, Palmyra and Rivanna Mills.

The 1828 field notebook of the engineer Claudius Crozet has sketch-maps of the seven lock sites, and of another lock and canal at Wood's Mill near Columbia.

At that time the most important port on the upper Rivanna was opposite Charlottesville at the mouth of Moore's Creek. Charlottesville called itself "the Athens of the South" and named its port Pireus, as the ancient Greeks had done.

EARLY MILLDAMS IN FLUVANNA

The milldam for Union Mills was the first on the river below the Albemarle line, built by John Bowie Magruder in 1796. Then John Ashlin erected his dam for Rivanna Mills in 1809, Walker and John Timberlake secured the permit for theirs at Palmyra in 1813, and William Wood made a millpond just west of Columbia early in the century.

When there was enough water in the river, and when the locks and dams were in order, batteaux could travel at least 51 miles along the Rivanna and its forks. Tolls for using the company's navigation were payable at Rivanna Mills, and from Columbia batteaux could continue down the James River 56 more miles to Richmond.

MEADOWCROFT FAMILY

WING DAMS BETWEEN CROFTON AND BROKEN ISLAND. Built at an angle to the bank, like a wing, these stone structures directed the river into a navigable channel. Wing dams on the Rivanna aided batteau navigation.

21

"I am ready to cut my dam in any place, and at any moment requisite, so as to remove that impediment if it be thought one, and to leave those interested to make the most of the natural circumstances of the place. [B]ut I hope they will never take from me my canal, made thro' the body of my own lands . . . ."

3

THOMAS JEFFERSON AND THE RIVANNA COMPANY

Canals were the technical marvels of Jefferson's time, and he was particularly interested in them. For example, while he was ambassador to France in 1787, he took an eight-day voyage along one of Europe's most famous waterways, the Canal du Midi, and sent a technical report to George Washington. In typical Jeffersonian style he took his carriage off its wheels and placed it on the barge towed by horses. When he was tired of walking on the towpath, he retired to his carriage with its windows all around and wrote letters. He even attempted to introduce a new type of lock sluice-gate to the canal officials that would have saved the lockkeepers effort and time, but evidently his suggestion was not acted upon.

Another relic of his stay in France is a rough diagram on the back of a letter showing a boat passing through a flight of two connected locks. Later Jefferson had his own flight of three connected locks on his mill canal near Monticello.

In 1802, while he was President, Jefferson planned an enormous ship lock in the Washington, D.C., Navy Yard that would lift warships into a drydock where they could be preserved between wars. Jefferson was ridiculed for his visionary scheme, and the lock was never built; but Benjamin Henry Latrobe produced a beautiful drawing and a model was displayed in the White House. Another doomed design was a military canal that Jefferson and Colonel William Tatum proposed in 1813 between Norfolk and Lynnhaven Inlet at the mouth of the Chesapeake

METAL STRAP NEAR JEFFERSON'S MILL.
Tie up your boat and stay awhile.

JEFFERSON'S SHADWELL MILLS. He built these on his Shadwell estate on the site of the mill constructed by his father, c. 1757. No archeological studies have been done to locate the locks in Jefferson's canal, which were to the right of the picture. (First published in the 1853 Harper's New Monthly Magazine.)

Bay, on the premise that it would be helpful in case of enemy blockades.

JEFFERSON'S MILLS AND CANALS

On the Rivanna near Monticello, Jefferson built his own dam, lock and canal for his grain mills and textile factory. His corn and wheat mills were merchant mills that bought grain from farmers and shipped meal and flour downriver. Jefferson's father had built a mill there about 1757 with a half-mile canal, but it washed away in the Great Flood of 1771. Jefferson built on the same site, but "on a larger & safer scale" with a longer millrace.

From 1776 until it was finished in 1803, he spent over $20,000 and a great deal of time on this mill canal, most of which had to be blasted out of solid rock. At first his canal was not big enough to take batteaux. For the convenience of riparian owners shipping grain downstream of his mill, Jefferson offered to provide a batteau small enough to fit the canal. In fact, however, he spent yet more money on the canal, widening it to accommodate river batteaux.

Although the public-spirited Jefferson wanted to further navigation in any way he could after the Rivanna Company was formed, he was often at odds with them. When the Rivanna Company proposed to use his canal for navigation, his loyalties were divided between navigation and his mills. In many letters he wrote to the directors of the Rivanna Company, he offered compromises.

One letter written in 1810 is most interesting, for he gives us a picture of his river: ". . . my milldam & canal present a dead sheet of water from the entrance of the river into the mountains at Secretary's ford, to its exit at my mill."

His letter to the "gentlemen Directors" continues:

> . . . *[you] desire the use of my dam, to keep the back water in it's [sic] present navigable state. use it. I shall maintain it for my own purposes.*
> "*but we wish to raise [the dam] two feet.*" *then you must maintain the dam yourselves because being raised to 5 f[t]. it will be carried away [by floods] 10. times for once if it remains at 3. feet.*
> "*then we will not raise it, but we wish to use your*

canal." you are welcome to it.

"But we must widen it for batteaux." you are free to widen it but as admitting a greater volume of water will certainly destroy the bank in some places, you must maintain the bank.

"agreed, but we shall want a site for our lock at the lower end." I give it to you.

"timber earth & stone to build it." I give to you all common timber. fine timber trees must be paid for.

"agreed. we want a site & timber for our toll house." I give them to you.

"but while we are widening the canal, we must stop your mills, perhaps for a month." you may do it & I will charge nothing for the rent . . . .

During this period, 1811–1812, the Rivanna Company closed Jefferson's sluice at Milton Falls, replacing it with another. They also built a flight of three wooden locks near his mills at the lower end of his canal to connect to the river. His trouble with the locks started as soon as they were erected: They leaked badly, and wasted so much water that his mill had to shut down almost every time a boat passed through. By 1819 he said the locks were "ruinous and completely rotten."

Thanks to Jefferson, we have a map of the area as it was, which he drew to illustrate a long letter covering the history of his work on the river and his problems with the Rivanna Company.

The three lock chambers were probably of wood with stone wall backing, similar to those later built downstream. In 1817, anxious that they be improved, Jefferson made a remarkable architectural drawing of a flight of three connected locks, giving dimensions of the lock chambers and gates, the lift of each lock, and other building specifications. In drawing these plans Jefferson was ahead of his time, calling for structures built of stone, not wood. His plans were probably never executed, but all traces of his locks are now underground, so we will never know until archeologists study the site.

It is easy to sympathize with Jefferson in his struggle to see justice done, and to wonder why the company ignored his expert advice.

RUIN AT THE SITE OF JEFFERSON'S MILL (1976). There was a corner fireplace in this section of the wall.

WARREN ANDERSON

"*We are miserably circumstanced [here] as to the disposal of our wheat. [W]e can neither manufacture or sell it . . . tho we have fine mill seats at the head of the navigation of the Rivanna, we cannot get mills built . . . .*"

Th: Jefferson

(1793)

4

THE RIVANNA NAVIGATION COMPANY: LOCKS AND DAMS FOR BATTEAUX, 1827–1850

After Jefferson's death in 1826, others continued to improve the navigation on the Rivanna, men such as John H. Cocke, Walker Timberlake, Chastain Cocke, John Randolph Bryan, boat captains, mill owners and farmers. As trade on the river increased, the sluice system became inadequate. The sluices tended to drain the ponds above them, producing even shallower water, and batteaux often smashed against the wing dams while trying to shoot the rapids. This system aggravated the already existing problem of recurring low water levels: batteaux could travel fully laden only during freshets, when water was up.

The authorities decided to build a safer, more reliable navigation by constructing a number of new locks and dams, and by making improvements at the old milldams. The new company planned to provide the batteaux with a slack water system formed by a series of dams and locks, each dam backing water upstream to the next dam and lock. Jefferson would have been pleased.

The new company, the Rivanna Navigation Company, secured a charter from the state in 1827, and replaced the old Rivanna Company. In 1831 the state invested in the company through the Virginia Board of Public Works and construction began in earnest.

James Clark was the president of this new company in 1832 and was succeeded by W.H. Meriwether (by 1836), Colonel Thomas Macon (in 1843), and Thomas Jefferson Randolph (by 1851).

Claudius Crozet, Principal Engineer of the Virginia Board

FLUVANNA COUNTY DEED BOOK

SEAL OF THE RIVANNA NAVIGATION COMPANY. The document at top is the only known example of this seal with its stylized depiction of a boat [shown in black-on-white above]. The document was signed by John Randolph Bryan of Carysbrook Plantation, Fluvanna County. Bryan was godson of U.S. Senator John Randolph of Roanoke.

of Public Works in this period, made a new survey of the Rivanna and concluded, "The system of improvement which I think most eligible on this river, is that by locks and dams, adapted to the use of light steam-boats." However, the only steamboat that ever plied the Rivanna navigation came decades later, the innovative project of Chastain C. Cocke.

Owners of milldams on any river designated a "Public Highway" were required by law to have a lock to let boats through, yet milldams were a problem on the Rivanna. As Jefferson's experience had demonstrated, mixing navigation and milling was not an ideal situation, even though the milldams conveniently backed up water to the depth required by loaded boats.

A major problem: both mills and boats needed water, and when the river flow was low there was not enough to both fill the locks and run the mills. Under the old company's regulation, the millers had the water rights; any water left over could be used for navigation. When the new company was formed, the legal situation was reversed and boat navigation came first. George Stillman of Rivanna Mills, delegate to the General Assembly from Fluvanna, prepared a long, well-reasoned paper in 1828, but the problem was never resolved to everyone's satisfaction. A slack-water navigation that depended on the deeper water created by millponds was a project fraught with adversity.

Another problem had to do with the sites chosen for mills. They were often built at the heads of rapids, so a milldam lock merely put boats down into the rocks. This often necessitated a canal that extended below the dam, with one or more locks.

Locks and Dams for Batteaux

The new lock and dam navigation from Charlottesville to the James River required 13 dams and 18 locks. The company's count includes five more locks than dams. Jefferson's canal had three; the others may have been guard locks at the canal entrances.

Five of the dams were old milldams already mentioned: Jefferson's at Shadwell, Campbell's (Buck Island), Union Mills, Palmyra, and Rivanna Mills. The other eight dams were new ones built by the company at Pireus (Moore's Creek), Milton, Stump Island, Bernardsburg, Broken Island (later called Pettit's Island), Strange's farm (Oakhill, across the river from Carysbrook Plantation), White Rock and Columbia.

The navigation company took over the maintenance of the locks at these dams, except that some of the new ones were to be the responsibility of the mill owners. Landowners later built mills using at least three of the new dams: Pireus, Milton and Broken Island.

Only one of the old locks and dams was abandoned by the new navigation: Wood's Mill lock and dam were inundated by the new Columbia lock and dam. Until recent years the remains of Wood's dam were clearly seen just below the Route 6 bridge over the Rivanna, but the mill canal was obliterated long ago by floods. The new batteau lock and dam near Columbia were built by John G. Hughes just a few yards upstream from the future site of the James River and Kanawha Canal aqueduct over the Rivanna.

LOCKS AND DAMS ON THE SOUTH FORK

When one adds the batteau locks on the South Fork, the total for the Rivanna navigation is 22, with an average lift of seven feet. During this time of rebuilding, sluices on the South Fork were also replaced by a series of locks and dams up to Hydraulic Mills. Two locks were built at Rio Mills. One was built at Broad Mossing, and one at the Three Islands.

According to tradition William H. Meriwether built the first mill at Rio. In 1837 this same Meriwether was president of the navigation company when he contracted to build a dam at the "New Bridge," erected at Rio in 1836 for the Charlottesville Turnpike, and to connect it with the river below by two locks. A thriving village grew at the New Bridge. Claudius Crozet visited the site in 1838 and noted that the dam was seven feet high; the two serial locks together would raise and lower boats 14 feet. He recommended that each lock be nine feet wide and 74 feet between the gates, for batteaux up to 65 feet long.

COLLECTION, ALBEMARLE COUNTY HISTORICAL SOCIETY

HYDRAULIC MILLS BRIDGE. The highway still crosses the Rivanna here—at the Charlottesville reservoir—and "Hydraulic" survives as a road name and place name. The 1929 flood, whose aftermath is pictured here, was not kind to bridges.

RIO MILLS. Rio Mills was a few miles downstream of Hydraulic Mills on the South Fork. At one time both were owned by Abraham Louis Hildebrand. Rio dam fed the millrace of Rio Mills, which stood on the bank of a creek below the dam, and batteaux navigated down the race and through two locks.

At one time Abraham Louis Hildebrand owned both the Rio Mills and the Hydraulic Mills, which stood upstream. The Hildebrand family rebuilt Rio Mills after they were destroyed by Union soldiers in 1864, and continued operation until 1925.

Albemarle folk pronounce "Rio" to rhyme with "Ohio," and the names for the sites of two other locks are also interesting: Broad Mossing Ford and the Three Islands. The lock at the Broad Mossing Ford is of special interest because it is the only one in Virginia that did not require a dam or a canal; a convenient outcropping rock made a natural dam. However, the ford itself, like all fords on the Rivanna and its tributaries, was a crib ford, not unlike the crib dams, being a fretwork of timbers filled with rocks.

There are no islands at Three Islands today, but then, over the years, hundreds of small islands in the Rivanna have come and gone. Banks silt up and are then washed away, even those 15 and 20 feet high. Often, this ruthless erosion uncovers a long-lost lock. River enthusiasts often find sites that were covered and then uncovered. The river is full of surprises.

DAMS

The dams on the Rivanna were "crib dams," built in a log cabin fashion; the cribs filled with rock and broken stones, and the fronts (the upstream side) made more or less watertight with close-fitting planking. Remains of the early dams reveal heart pine timbers, mortised together with wooden pegs, as seen today at a section of the 1813 dam at Palmyra. A similar arrangement of heart pine timbers is apparent in the 1850 dam at Palmyra (see Chapter 5): layers of timbers placed alternately across the current and in line with the flow, but the timbers facing downstream were placed at an angle, slanting upward at the downstream end.

Remains of the other dams are visible today, the rocks strewn in the riverbed; some timbers are still held to the bedrock by wrought-iron bolts.

BATTEAU LOCKS

The locks were lined with horizontal wooden planks bolted to wooden posts, with outside walls of rocks. They were constructed on a foundation of

FREE BRIDGE. This was the second structure to span the Rivanna at Charlottesville. Its name, derived from the fact that it bypassed a toll bridge, continued to be used for later bridges at this site. When the present crossing for Highway 250 was erected, stones from the piers, with mason marks on them, were saved for the city at the request of Virginia Canals and Navigations Society member W.E. Trout.

1813 DAM REMAINS AT PALMYRA. This glimpse of a section of crib construction reveals the heart pine timbers mortised together and held with wooden pegs (note lower left 2-inch hole and the mortise cut.) The crib was filled with rocks and the upstream side was covered with closely fitted boards to make it more nearly watertight.

heavy timbers, unless they were built on bedrock. The remains of these batteau locks on the Rivanna of this period are all much alike, and almost all agree with the construction suggested by Chief Engineer Crozet:

> *The locks which are necessarily to be made of wood, should consist of a foundation of cross sills laid on the ground on Longitudinal sleepers bolted to rock, as the case may require. On every other cross sill uprights 8 by 10 inches should be framed about three feet apart.*

Measurements of the locks at Milton, Bernardsburg (Crofton), Strange's (Oak Hill) and White Rock (near Carysbrook) show that they had two parallel walls eight feet apart, made of upright timbers every three feet, backed by stone walls and lined with horizontal planks. At Strange's the builders took advantage of a tall thin rock as part of the lock on the river side. At Strange's and at White Rock enough of each lock chamber is still visible to measure the length and both were big enough for batteaux up to 60 feet long, the same size as the batteau locks measured by Jefferson on his canal in 1817.

An 1823 legislative petition, preserved in the Library of Virginia, gives picturesque and revealing examples of trouble on the Rivanna navigation. John H. Craven, owner of a manufacturing mill above the town of Milton, reported trouble in the canal leading to Wood's dam and lock:

> *. . . in the winter of 1820 his . . . new boat, on her first trip loaded with flour & tobacco, which was detained 5 or 6 days in Wm. Wood's canal, his lock being out of order or impassable. That during this detention, the boat being in the canal, the bank gave way, fell upon his boat & sank it & his hands escaped with difficulty.*
>
> *[His produce was] so much injured as to be worth little or nothing, & the boat itself so much injured, as to be unfit for further navigation . . . .*

The petition concluded by saying that the locks and dams were not maintained properly by the mill owners, and were an obstruction to navigation, and that their boatmen were "bank-

ROBERT AND SANDY MEADOWCROFT

CROFTON BATTEAU LOCK. *Built in the 1830s, this lock, like the others on the Rivanna, had a chamber of planks nailed to upright posts spaced every three feet. Several posts are visible (arrows), as is a lining plank at the water line. The planks and posts were backed by large dry-laid stones. The remains here were preserved by the Virginia Department of Transportation when a new bridge for Route 600 was built in 1981.*

LEE STRUBLE

WHITE ROCK BATTEAU LOCK. *Note the iron rod, which held a wooden upright, to which the wooden lining was nailed.*

STRANGE'S BATTEAU LOCK. *At this old dam site the batteau FLUVANNA ventures into the remains of the old batteau lock. The builders adapted the natural outcropping bedrock as part of the lock wall. Posts that held the horizontal lining boards are still visible beyond this point and on the other side of the eight-foot-wide chamber.*

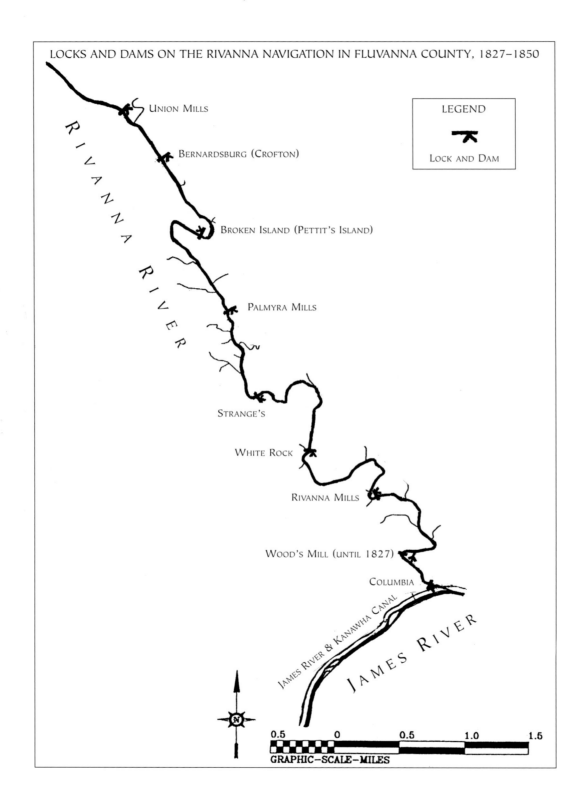

LOCKS AND DAMS ON THE RIVANNA NAVIGATION IN FLUVANNA COUNTY, 1827–1850

LEGEND

LOCK AND DAM

RIVANNA RIVER

UNION MILLS

BERNARDSBURG (CROFTON)

BROKEN ISLAND (PETTIT'S ISLAND)

PALMYRA MILLS

STRANGE'S

WHITE ROCK

RIVANNA MILLS

WOOD'S MILL (UNTIL 1827)

COLUMBIA

James River & Kanawha Canal

JAMES RIVER

N

0.5   0   0.5   1.0   1.5

GRAPHIC-SCALE-MILES

UNION MILLS FACTORY. Despite the troubles with the dams and the batteau locks of 1827–1850, mills on the Rivanna flourished, including the Union Mills Factory in upper Fluvanna. In 1835 Joseph Martin described Union Mills in his GAZETEER OF VIRGINIA: Located "in the midst of beautiful mountain and river scenery," the site included a merchant mill, grist mill and saw mill, and "The Union Factory . . . a large and commodious brick building; it runs 1500 spindles, besides the necessary machinery for carding, etc. It contains 12 power looms . . . in which several hundred yards of substantial cloth are made per day. More than 100 operatives are employed . . . ." The Magruder and Timberlake families ran these mills for many years.

rupt, ruined & driven off, by the Detention at these locks & forfeiture of freight by damage to cargoes in the portages around them . . . ."

The millowners replied in a petition of January 10, 1824, arguing that "it would seem that in the imagination of the petitioners those Dams & Locks are like Pandora's box—the fruitful source of every evil with which human nature can be visited, and if the existing laws were enforced, the locks would be kept in repair." They concluded by claiming the liquor shops along the river slowed the boatmen down, then stopped them entirely.

These issues notwithstanding, the Rivanna navigation system for batteaux survived another quarter of a century.

BOB GOOCH

"... I must observe that I hold the lands thro' which the navigation is to pass, under a purchase and grant from the crown, comprehending the bed of the river, across which the chain was stretched both above & below, that the bed of the river was estimated as part of the contents of the grant, for which the same price was paid as for other parts of the land . . . ."

Th:Jefferson

(1810)

5

LOCKS AND DAMS FOR HORSE-DRAWN CANAL BOATS, 1850–1854

In mid-century the Rivanna Navigation Company planned to replace the batteaux on the river with horse-drawn canal boats. When canals and towpaths were built, the batteaux were in part replaced by large horse- and mule-drawn canal boats. However, one cannot speak simply of a batteau era and a canal era in Virginia, for even after towpaths were built on a few rivers, batteaux continued to run. Many of them came down the smaller rivers, transferred their loads to canal boats, or made their way to Richmond on the canal. Only four navigations in the state ever had towpaths for horse-drawn boats: the James River, two of its tributaries—the Maury (North River) and the Rivanna—and the Dismal Swamp Canal. Thus the batteau era of man-powered boats extended long into the canal era of horse-drawn boats.

The James River and Kanawha Canal was completed from Richmond to Columbia in 1840, and to Lynchburg later that year. The locks on the new canal were 15 feet wide and would have been handy for Rivanna batteaux, for they could fit two abreast and save lockage time.

However, batteaux coming down the Rivanna could not go directly into the new James River canal at Columbia, because for ten years there was no direct connection between the two waterways. The James River canal crossed over the Rivanna by way of a beautiful three-arched dressed-stone aqueduct. The nearest water connection for Rivanna boats was a river lock at Cartersville, ten miles down the James.

The new canal on the James was a work of beauty, a bright ribbon of water circling the southern boundaries of Fluvanna and Albemarle, anchored by big stone locks. It brought a different style of transportation. Large mule-drawn freight boats

RIVANNA AQUEDUCT AT COLUMBIA, 1840–1944. Built to carry the James River and Kanawha Canal over the Rivanna, it was the canal's longest aqueduct, featuring three cut-stone arches. After canal days it accommodated trains, as well as wagons and cars. The Chesapeake & Ohio Railroad blew it up in 1944, and only the west abutment remains.

laden with produce or merchandise, and horse-drawn passenger (packet) boats bearing travelers, luggage, mail and parcels passed over the Rivanna on the sturdy stone aqueduct, bound for Richmond or points to the west.

It was the packet boats gliding up and down the canal beside the James that people remembered with such fondness, and many who had been passengers on these floating hotels wrote about their travels with romantic nostalgia. There never has been a mode of transportation so serene, so calm and smooth. Such a comfortable means of travel; the passengers were not jolted, nor were they tossed from side to side. No roar of an engine, just a leisurely drifting, the silence broken only by the boat horn as they approached a lock, the clip-clop of the horses' feet and the music of songbirds. The passengers viewed the scenery, visited, and enjoyed the bountiful meals. (Some noted the sleeping arrangements were not always the most comfortable!)

Some sources claim the Rivanna Navigation Company owned one canal passenger packet boat; the most specific record found of a packet boat on the Rivanna states that a young lady named Fanny boarded a packet at Rivanna Mills on Christmas Eve, 1858 and went down the Rivanna and the James to Manakin's Ferry (ticket, $1.50).

This great feat of engineering—the James River and Kanawha Canal—made the Rivanna navigation out of date, with batteau locks much too small for the big canal freighters 93 feet long, and no towpath for mules or horses. According to its charter the Rivanna Navigation Company was obliged to upgrade its works once the James River and Kanawha Canal reached Fluvanna County. However, the company did not immediately respond to the challenge.

Petitions were sent to the General Assembly from groups who opposed the improvements and from those who heartily endorsed them. Investment in the navigation was already too great to be thrown away at that time. Shippers on the Rivanna depended on it to get produce to market, and they did not want to give it up, even though the Virginia Central Railroad had already planned its route, and the rails would reach Charlottesville by 1850. So, then as now, "progress and improvements" won the day, and the Rivanna navigation was rebuilt once more.

The James River and Kanawha Company engineers surveyed the Rivanna to plan the new works, which included seven large stone locks, six miles of canals, 20 miles of towpaths, and two new dams: at Carysbrook and at Rivanna Mills. When the new dams were built, Carysbrook replaced Strange's lock and dam, and the dam at Rivanna Mills was so high it flooded White Rock lock and dam.

The companies at first planned to extend the improvements all the way to Jefferson's Mill site and Charlottesville, but the upper Rivanna, in Albemarle County, was never fully developed for towpath navigation. As far as we know, large mule-drawn canal boats could never go farther upstream than the upper reaches of the pond made by the dam at Union

Mills: that is, to the Albemarle-Fluvanna line at Thrift's Ford, eight miles from Charlottesville. One source states that by 1857 boats of "50 tons burden" could reach a point five miles from Charlottesville, therefore near Jefferson's mill site. However, except for a wall at Stump Island, no large navigation structures have been found on this section of the river.

HARPERS WEEKLY, MAY 14, 1870. REPRINTED BY JOSEPH W. BLILEY. COLOR ADDED.

CANAL FREIGHT BOAT. This illustration shows many similarities to a Rivanna canal freight boat, with passengers, a steersman, a man in the bow, and a "hogee" walking with two mules.

The Rivanna remained a slack-water navigation (one dam and lock backed water to the next dam and lock), though there were short segments of canal, and a towpath was built the length of the river in Fluvanna. Like those on the James, the new locks were 15 feet wide and 100 feet long in the chambers, for boats up to 93 feet long and 14½ feet wide. Canal freight boat navigation became possible.

The old batteau locks were abandoned, and those at Broken Island and Rivanna Mills were destroyed by the 1850 construction. Those at Union Mills, Bernardsburg, and Columbia were bypassed by new canals, and those at Palmyra, Strange's and White Rock were inundated by the new millponds, so more remains of these last three have survived.

The new works of the 1850s on the Rivanna were—and still are—magnificent structures, built to last for centuries. In charge of building them was engineer John Couty, "of whom no higher compliment can be paid than by simply saying the floods of the seasons have passed over his work in every possible stage of construction, without displacing the first stick or stone that has been laid down."

John Couty's stonework on the Rivanna is among the best in the state and is the most complete of the preserved navigation systems in Virginia. The nine locks are of carefully shaped granite masonry. The stones that lined the lock chambers were dressed until they were perfectly smooth, while others were "hammer dressed" (by pounding with a big hammer) to a relatively flat but dimpled surface. They provided both a pleasing appearance and a smooth wall that did not damage boats rubbing against it.

By comparison, the other stones usually were left with a rougher "quarry faced" surface, and those on the back of the walls, which were covered with earth, had an even rougher finish. (Types of stonework can easily be seen at the Palmyra lock.) Many of the stone blocks are as large as four feet by six, and one can barely imagine the intensity of labor required to raise them to such heights and to place them, row upon row.

These locks have wooden foundations, wooden floors and wood-capped miter sills for the gates. Both mitered gates pointed upstream. They were immense, each half built with a huge metal sluice gate, weighing about 200 pounds, near the bottom. When raised, this sluice gate allowed the lock to empty or fill slowly. Each half-gate was topped with a massive wooden beam, and once the water pressure was equal on both sides of the gate, a man could easily cantilever the gate, swinging it back into its niche in the walls of the lock.

As a boat captain approached a lock, he blew a big horn to let the lockkeeper know he needed the lock gates opened. The call of that horn echoed through the hills and fields, breaking the monotony of farm chores with its call, a reminder of faraway places.

The most northern of these locks was constructed at Union Mills across the river from the old batteau lock and the mills. Downstream from this lock, a canal with a towpath was dug and leveled along the southwest bank of the river down to the two locks at Bernardsburg. This two miles of canal bypassed the old dam and the batteau locks on the other shore. At the end of the canal the boats entered first a "lift-lock," then a boat basin, and then a river lock, to go back into the river in water that was made deeper by the next dam down-

LOCK STONEWORK OF 1850. Three different kinds of stonework can be seen at the Palmyra lock: Smooth-dressed stones can be seen on the inside walls near the gate recess; at lower left are rougher stones for the abutment. The roughest quarry-faced stones front the river.

STONE STEPS. The lock at Palmyra was higher at its upstream end, to protect against floods. These steps still lead up to the higher part. Note drill holes in stones on the river side.

RESTORED LOCK ON THE JAMES. The only restored canal boat lock in Virginia, similar to those Couty built on the Rivanna, was reconstructed by the National Park Service where the Blue Ridge Parkway crosses the James. Its wooden gates were copied from buried ones. Note the long cantilevered beams, which were used to open and shut the lock gates.

QUARRYING FOR STONE. Drill holes remain from splitting squared stones from the cliff at Buzzard's Rock, just above Rivanna Mills. Similar drill marks can also be seen on the stones in the locks.

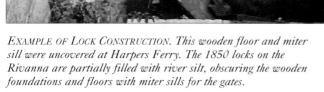

EXAMPLE OF LOCK CONSTRUCTION. This wooden floor and miter sill were uncovered at Harpers Ferry. The 1850 locks on the Rivanna are partially filled with river silt, obscuring the wooden foundations and floors with miter sills for the gates.

CHARLES P. JONES

LOCK GATE STRAPS. The metal and stone to hold a lock gate's swivel post can still be seen on several Rivanna locks. LEFT: Iron straps wrapped around the post, holding it at the top. MIDDLE RIGHT: The straps were attached by iron anchors atop the coping stones. MIDDLE LEFT: Stones curved to fit around the post were called hollow quoin stones; the lock at Rivanna Mills is the only one on the Rivanna with quoin stones to fit around the post from top to bottom. BOTTOM: Illustration of lock gate of the type used on the Rivanna and the James, with cantilevered beams.

CHARLES M. WINKLER

NATIONAL PARK SERVICE

river at Broken Island. At this dam and lock, boats again entered a canal, for one mile, to another river lock at Dog Point. Here boats slipped into the river deepened by the millpond at Palmyra Mills. At Palmyra the towpath changed from the southwest bank to the opposite shore and continued on the northeast side; the mules and horses crossed the river on the covered bridge.

After passing through the Palmyra lock, the boats floated downriver in the deep water backed from the Carysbrook dam. The Carysbrook lock lowered the boats

SKETCH BY W.E. TROUT

UNION MILLS LOCK. The Rivanna's "unique" lock was cut through a scenic cliff on its west bank, so that part of the lock chamber was cut stone and another part the existing bedrock. Still another part, apparently, was a wooden wall. Photo above shows the unusual lock wall, of cut stone and bedrock, which corresponds to the wall at the right of the sketch.

UNION MILLS DAM. The photograph shows the dam essentially as it was rebuilt in 1850. The lock is on the west (i.e., near) side, the mills on the east. This picture shows the timber cribbing, which was filled with rock; the front or upstream face of the crib was covered with planking to further resist water. Only a few timbers in the rapids can be seen now.

Union Mills Lock, on the Rivanna Navigation — TROUT '66

GIFT OF B.F.D. RUNK TO THE OLD STONE JAIL MUSEUM

into slack water created by the new dam and lock at Rivanna Mills, and at this lock the James River and Kanawha Company and the Rivanna Navigation Company joined in the building of a canal for 4½ miles to Columbia, called "the Rivanna Connexion." Like the canal below Union Mills, the towpath was on the river side of the canal. At Columbia there is a special lock that joined the two canals, and there the boats entered the James River and Kanawha Canal.

DAMS, LOCKS AND SHORT CANALS

UNION MILLS TO COLUMBIA

The sites of the wooden crib dams on the Rivanna are clearly delineated in the bed of the river today, with rocks and timbers still visible. They were about 24 feet thick from front to back. Now their remains create interesting white water for canoeists.

Each lock has many small and interesting differences. One cannot say of the Rivanna, "If you've seen one lock you've seen them all." And the river's floods and years of drought keep making changes, so that there is always something new to discover.

UNION MILLS DAM AND LOCK

The stone of the lock at Union Mills is still perfectly intact. It is unique. Part of the chamber was cut from the "living rock" of the hemlock-covered cliff. The walls of smooth-dressed blocks of stone give way on both sides to sections of the rough native stone of the cliff, a variation in construction that may have chafed the sides of boats. One section against the cliff may have been built of wood, for there is an alcove in the lock today. The rock cliff towers above this sample of Couty's work, and the sun never reaches to the ferns, squirrel corn and star of Bethlehem that line the bed of the lock.

UNION MILLS CANAL TO CROFTON

A short section of the towpath and canal below the lock has been destroyed by a farm road, and for the length of a field the towpath has been leveled beside the ditch of the

UPPER CROFTON LOCK. Built to lift or lower boats in the Union Mills Canal, this lock's stonework is the most exposed on the Rivanna. Note the low "breastwall" at the upper end—the "stairstep." Residents of Lake Monticello, led by Al Sullivan, have kept the walls clean of silt and have maintained a trail on the old towpath, up to Route 600.

LOWER CROFTON LOCK. This river lock lies so low that silt from floods usually keeps it covered. A troop of Boy Scouts—Post 101 from Cunningham Church—used shovels and wheelbarrows to uncover the coping stones so that the lock could be measured.

canal, but, from that point, the canal and towpath are almost intact for 2½ miles down to the next lock. The towpath beside the canal presents a wonderful opportunity for a hiking trail for the Lake Monticello development. There are three modern cuts through the canal near the Lake Monticello dam: one for the spillway, one for Route 600, and a third below the lake's dam.

So steep was the fall of the river that two stone locks were needed at the lower end of the Union Mills Canal at Crofton. The northern one is the most exposed lock on the river, with less silt in the chamber. There was a boat basin between the two locks.

The lower lock was a river or outlet lock, lowering the boats down into the river. This lock lies

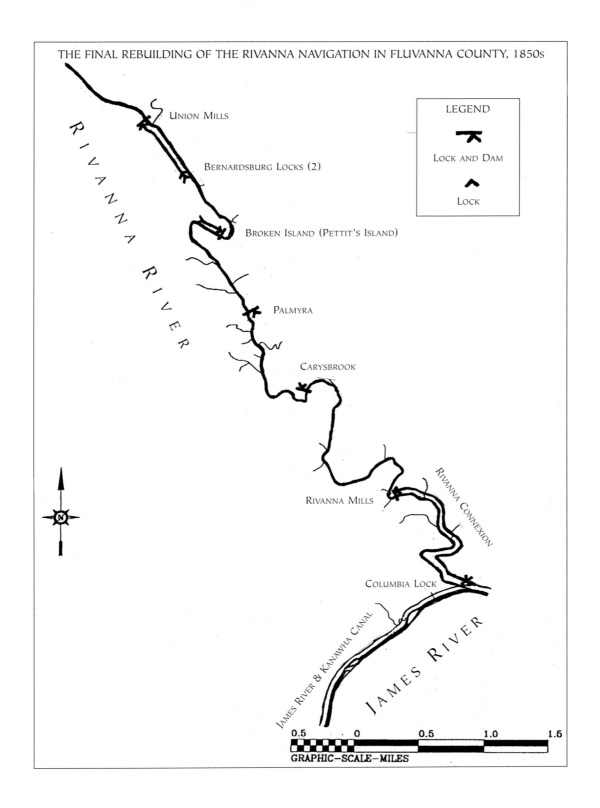

THE FINAL REBUILDING OF THE RIVANNA NAVIGATION IN FLUVANNA COUNTY, 1850s

LEGEND

Lock and Dam

Lock

Union Mills

Bernardsburg Locks (2)

Broken Island (Pettit's Island)

Palmyra

Carysbrook

Rivanna Mills

Rivanna Connexion

Columbia Lock

James River & Kanawha Canal

James River

Rivanna River

GRAPHIC-SCALE-MILES

PETE RUNGE

UPPER BROKEN ISLAND LOCK. This lock was built of stone at each of the four corners where the gates were located. The chamber between the gates was probably lined with wood, but no remnants of stone or wooden sides have yet been found. Members of the VC&NS were clearing the trees and other growth from this lock.

so low that floods keep it covered with river silt. When a troop of Boy Scouts uncovered the coping stones of the lock in 1996, it was the first time in over 80 years those blocks had seen the light of day. Floods soon covered them again.

BROKEN ISLAND
(PETTIT'S ISLAND) LOCK

The lock at the end of the Broken Island dam is not at all like the others on the Rivanna and is a puzzle today. There are stone lock-gate sections at each end: each corner of the lock, at the gates, is of cut stone, but between those stone structures are only dirt embankments. Canal enthusiasts studying the site presumed that the earthen sides contained the remains of wood-faced stone walls. However, recent archaeological study has so far revealed no stone or timbers,

ALL THAT'S LEFT OF THE LOCKKEEPER'S HOUSE. This chimney beside the lower lock of the Broken Island canal is the only remains of a lock house that has been found along the Rivanna. An archeological examination of the site is in progress.

so at this time we must conclude that the water in the lock was contained by earthen levees.

The name Broken Island appears in the earliest records, and the navigation dam, lock and canal bore that name. In time the island was renamed for a new owner and became Pettit's Island, and highway maps erroneously placed the old name on a much smaller island upstream. For many years in the twentieth century, corn was grown on Broken Island.

The mile-long canal between the lock at the dam and the river lock is the most delightful walk; because of a large "S" curve in the Rivanna, the river flows on your right and the

COURTESY JONES MEMORIAL LIBRARY, LYNCHBURG, VA.

OVERTON McGEHEE

1850 DAM AND LOCK AT PALMYRA. Both the 1813 and 1850 dams were of "crib dam" construction, as seen in a photograph (UPPER LEFT) from the archives of the Chesapeake & Ohio Railroad shows the dismantling of Coleman's Dam on the James River. ABOVE: When the Rivanna is low, one can clearly see the heart pine timbers of the 1850 Palmyra crib dam. LEFT: The Palmyra lock, seen in August 2001.

curving earthwork of the towpath is on your left. The trees arch overhead, with no obstructing undergrowth, and sometimes the canal is filled with water. The outlet lock lies very low, but Virginia Canals and Navigations Society workers have been uncovering it.

PALMYRA

The remains of three separate dams are found at Palmyra today. The Rivanna was first dammed there in 1813. The county justices gave the Timberlake brothers, Walker and

John, Jr., permission to build a dam across the Rivanna to provide water power for their mills. (Reverend Walker Timberlake chose the name of his mills from the Bible. Old Tadmor in Syria was called Palmyra by the Romans.) The records state the dam would be built just above the Solitude Spring Branch, and that is just where the remains of that first dam are today.

Flood waters recently uncovered much more of the 1813 dam, and the rocks at the southwest abutment and the lock at the opposite end are clearly visible. The wonderful big heartpine timbers of the crib for this dam can be seen when the river is low.

At low flows the remains of a dam also can be seen between the remaining big midstream pier of the covered bridge and the northeast bank. No lock site is visible today. Since no record of such a dam has been found, one wonders if this was a partial or a cofferdam.

More of the 1850 dam at the dressed-stone lock at Palmyra has survived than of any other on the Rivanna, leading to the theory that this dam was unusually well built, and perhaps was the last one to break.

The dam abutment on the southwest bank is still intact, and on the stones of the two abutments and on the inner lock walls are found mason's marks chiseled by the stone masons who dressed them. These are found on several of the navigation structures on the Rivanna. Much of the manual labor on the navigation was performed by African-American slaves.

In the 1850 rebuilding, the navigation company used 16½ acres of land on the southwest side of the river, the farm of the Noel family, for the deeper millpond and for

CHARLES M. WINKLER

SPECIAL GATE. The Palmyra lock was the Rivanna's only lock with a "stop-gate" at the upstream end. Planks could be slipped into grooves to block the water flow while the gates were repaired. Note the round indentations in the stones for the use of huge tongs in lifting the stones.

DRAWINGS BY W.E. TROUT

MASON'S MARKS AT PALMYRA. Marks chiseled into stones by the masons who dressed them are found on both the east and west abutments of the Palmyra dam as well as in the lock walls. Similar marks are found on several other navigation structures along the Rivanna.

51

HUCK FINN DAYS AT PALMYRA. Children fish near the stone lock. Behind is the broken dam (which broke c. 1915) and the covered bridge.

the towpath approaching Palmyra. The millpond was so big that there was an acre island in the pond where a farmer raised corn. Downriver of Palmyra the property needed for the navigation was all deeded to the navigation company, but much of the necessary land north of Palmyra was condemned. We do not know if the landowners on the west side upriver were unwilling to deed the parcels to the navigation company, but there was a reason the engineers wanted to go up the west bank instead of continuing up the east side: There were only very small streams to cross on the west bank, while on the east they would have to build an aqueduct for the Union Mills Canal over a much larger creek, Mechunk.

Since the towpath crossed the river at Palmyra, the mules were unhitched to cross over by the covered bridge. From the millpond the boats entered the lock on the northeast side.

CARYSBROOK DAM. In the 1850 rebuilding of the navigation, John Randolph Bryan of Carysbrook Plantation persuaded the company to abandon the Strange and White Rock batteau locks and build this dam, where Bryan later built Carysbrook Mill. The lock was located on the opposite bank, at Oak Hill Plantation.

When the water level was very low, the slackwater from the Carysbrook dam did not reach the outlet of this lock. Walker Timberlake asked permission to cut a canal below it, but there is no evidence it was ever built. Walter Payne, who had ridden the boats, said that when there was not enough water below the lower gates, the lock chamber was filled again to its deepest level. The lockkeeper then let this water rush out, and the boat floated downriver on this tide.

CARYSBROOK LOCK, DAM AND MILL

The owner of Carysbrook Plantation persuaded the navigation company to replace the White Rock dam with one behind his mansion so he could have a small mill there. The lock is on the Oak Hill side of the river, all the structures part of the 1850

CARYSBROOK LOCK. *This stonework was located on the Oak Hill Plantation side of the river (i.e., the northeast), opposite the Carysbrook Mill and the long dam abutment.*

LUCY MITCHELL HOLLAND BERTOLETT

CARYSBROOK MILL. *This small mill, built by John Randolph Bryan when a navigation dam was constructed near his home, was patronized by the neighborhood.*

improvements. Boats going downstream approached this lock in a short canal that cut across a field in a sweeping curve of the river. After the lock was abandoned, the upper gate was used as a form for a cement barrier to stop flood water in the canal. River silt has filled the canal and the low-ground field is no longer divided. As late as 1950 the trace of the canal could be seen on an aerial photograph.

Flood waters removed the earth on the west bank and revealed the outer stone wall of the lock braced with a rough stone buttress. A later flood brought logs to batter the buttress and tore away the top of this support.

RIVANNA CONNEXION CANAL. The Rivanna Navigation and the James River and Kanawha Canal companies connected the two navigations by means of a 4½-mile canal from Rivanna Mills to the Columbia lock.

RIVANNA MILLS

The navigation structures at Rivanna Mills were completely rebuilt by the James River and Kanawha and Rivanna companies. A canal for boats beginning at Buzzard's Rock was cut across a curve in the river, bypassing the old dam and bringing water to the mill and the new lock. The new dam—an incredible (for this region) 19 feet tall—was so close to the mills that one miller claimed it caused much more flooding in the buildings than they had suffered before. (Only at Palmyra and Rivanna Mills did the mill and the lock use the same supply canal; at other dam sites the lock was on the opposite bank.)

1850 DAM AT RIVANNA MILLS (ABOVE). An incredible 19 feet high, the roar of its falling water could be heard for miles.

JOHN COUTY'S PLAT FOR RIVANNA MILLS (LEFT). The engineer's drawing shows the rebuilding of the dam, lock, and canals. A short boat canal, beginning below Buzzard's Rock, brought boats to a new guard lock. This channel bypassed the old dam, but a feeder canal brought water from the new millpond. (Note site of old lock.) Just below the new lock was a boat basin and the beginning of the new Rivanna Connexion Canal. The "Proposed Bridge" later carried the Bryant Ford Road to a water-level bridge across the river.

CHARLES P. JONES

CULVERTS ON THE RIVANNA CONNEXION CANAL. The only stone-arched culverts along the Rivanna are both found on the Connexion Canal, carrying Dog Creek (ABOVE) and Gum Creek (RIGHT) under the canal and towpath. Both culverts are 90 feet long and tall enough for a person to walk through. The towpath and canal above the culverts are constructed of earth.

There is so little fill at the upper end of this lock that part of the metal of the gate is sometimes visible. Now that no boats wait impatiently to use this lock, white violets have carpeted its bank to lure explorers to this historic site, bypassed by time but sturdily enduring.

However, it was the Rivanna Connexion Canal that stirred the imagination of Fluvanna folk in 1850 and that gives a true

STONE BOX CULVERT (ABOVE). Pictured on the north side of the Bryant Ford Road, it is a marvel, a very long square culvert that still carries a stream under the road, canal and towpath to the river.

FARM ROAD OVERPASS, RIVANNA CONNEXION (RIGHT). These are the only remains of a bridge over a canal identified in Fluvanna County. The towpath curved behind this embankment. The mule was unhitched to continue along the towpath, the rope was tossed to the boatman, the boat continued drifting under the bridge, then the rope was tossed back and the mule rehitched, all in seconds. Maintaining such farm bridges was a major expense for the canal company.

glimpse of the past. The canal, built by the two companies to connect the Rivanna navigation with the James River Canal, began at the boat basin below the new lock and dam and ran 4½ miles to Columbia, with two small cut-stone aqueducts over the creeks. At St. Andrews Street in Columbia, a special junction lock let boats into the James River and Kanawha Canal.

COLUMBIA JUNCTION LOCK

In the lock at St. Andrews Street, the mitered gates face in different directions with only 35 feet between the gates, though the lock is long and disappears under the old street. (The company would have built a bridge for the street.) In the 1960s we found no one who had any knowledge of how the Rivanna Connexion Canal and the James River canal joined. Too many years had passed since the demise of the James River Canal. In the memories of the Columbia folk, the Rivanna Canal continued east beside the railroad embankment (the old towpath), passed under the Columbia railroad station beside the tracks, and ended just below, near Route 6.

Extant records did not help our understanding, except that a plat for the Rivanna Canal, drawn by Couty, shows a boat basin above the lock. When the Rivanna Connexion Canal was

OVERTON McGEHEE

TOWPATH AND CANAL. Near Route 6, west of Columbia, the towpath and the Rivanna Connexion canal are intact for one-half mile above St. Andrews Street. In some seasons, rainwater gives the canal the appearance of having been restored.

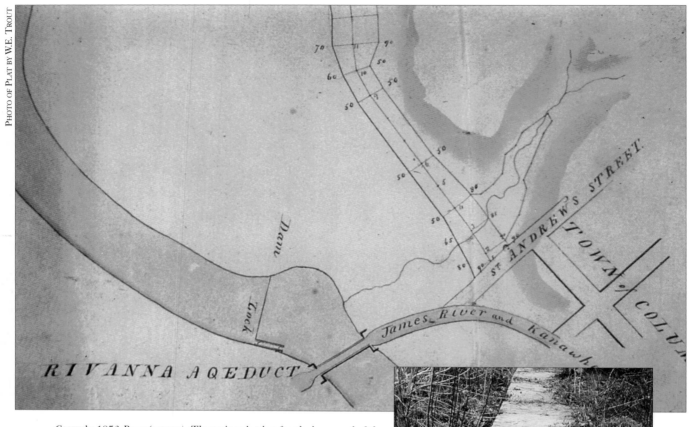

COUTY'S 1850 PLAT (ABOVE). The engineer's plan for the lower end of the Rivanna Connexion canal offers no clue as to how the Rivanna navigation was to be joined to the James River and Kanawha Canal.

1850 COLUMBIA JUNCTION LOCK (RIGHT). The stonework lies partially under St. Andrews Street, at the end of the Rivanna Connexion canal. This lock marks the junction of the Rivanna navigation and the James River and Kanawha Canal. Excavation indicates that the lock chamber was 35 feet in length, between two gates that faced in opposite directions—the only junction lock of this type in Virginia.

completed about 1851, the water level in the canals was equal, and we can only surmise that these gates were for convenience in repairing either waterway. Or it would prevent a flood on either canal flowing over into the other.

Once a Rivanna boat cleared this lock, a smooth ride to Richmond lay ahead, on a navigation system that went far beyond Jefferson's plans of just 30 to 40 years before.

WARREN ANDERSON

PICNIC, ANYONE? Approaching Stump Island Dam.

". . . I am sorry it is not in my power to give you any information how far the making [of] a dam across the Rivanna might interfere with the rights of the James river company." [To Robert Quarles, Point of Fork.]

(1809)

6

NAVIGATION NUMBERS

In 1848, the Rivanna Navigation Company listed the equipment it owned: "two yoke of oxen, a saw mill and [blank] acres of land, six Negro men, carpenter's tools, one oxcart and two boats and utensils." According to tradition the company's sawmill and boatyard were near the Broken Island locks at a place known as Lane's. On the east side, not far from the dam, there was a port and store called Flanagan's Landing, a commercial site replaced by Wildwood Station and store on the railroad in 1908. A woods road still leads to the Flanagan homesite.

The Rivanna management invested over $200,000 in new locks and dams between 1851 and 1857. The new horse- and mule-drawn navigation of the 1850s brought large, modern canal boats to Fluvanna. The route traversed the county through its center, a distance of 27 miles. Research and recent discoveries of sunken boats suggest that smaller boats still plied the river higher up into Albemarle County to a point near Jefferson's Shadwell Mills (which in 1829 had passed into the hands of the Timberlake and Magruder families, who had operated the Union Mills).

Censuses of the period give successive glimpses of work on the navigation. In 1850, 27 men and one woman hired by the company produced stone worth $7,500; in 1860, 34 men were employed, but no value was given for the stone.

Ready means of transportation and the water power provided by the river encouraged the mill owners. The managers of Union Mills reported to the census of 1850 that their investment was $30,000 in the cotton factory, and that they employed 25 workers, purchased 225,000 pounds of raw material and produced yarn valued at $34,000. Their grain mill, with a $5,000 investment, bought 8,000 bushels of wheat and produced 1,775 barrels of flour, valued at $9,300. Their tannery produced leather valued at $1,000.

SOUTHSIDE AND RIVANNA CONNECTIONS.
DISBURSEMENTS, on the following accounts:

Southside connections:

Cartersville dam, - - - -			161 13
Bent Creek bridge, - -	70 48		
New Canton " - -	1,041 61		
Hardwicksville " - -	3,625 78		
Insurance on bridges, - -	300 00		
Hardwicksville lumberhouse, - -	42 55		
		5,241 55	

Rivanna connection:

Damages, - - -	143 00		
Pay of arbitrators, - -	38 00		
		181 00	
			5,422 55
Excess of disbursements over receipts, Oct. 1st, 1854, - -			106,794 55
Amount borrowed from improvements in operation, - -			**$ 112,217 10**

SUMMARY STATEMENT. James River and Kanawha Company, year ending 30 September 1855.

Rivanna Mills reported a capital investment in the mills of $12,000; they bought 114,000 bushels of wheat and produced flour valued at $17,000. In "off-seasons" the mill also ground tons of plaster (calcium to spread on cropland) for the farmers. Their reports reflect the work of the corn mill: 10,000 bushels of corn that year.

Boatbuilders in Fluvanna were busy in 1850: William Jones built ten boats, and William Anderson reported hiring nine men who built boats valued at $4,500. Later boatbuilders were Benjamin F. Childress and Wesley C. Tutwiler.

Account books of the 1850 decade reveal some names of freight boats that carried the Fluvanna tobacco, flour and farm produce to market and returned with merchandise for homes and farms: *Oronoco*, *Phoenix* and *Rainbow*. Account books for the Union Mills carried many entries for a boat called the *Star of Albemarle*, and a few entries for the *Don Pedro*. We like to think that Jefferson, who had first explored the Rivanna in a canoe and had shipped the yield of his mills and farms on undependable batteaux, would have been proud of the *Star of Albemarle*.

Between 1830 and 1850 Fluvanna had enjoyed unprecedented prosperity from the cultivation of a very hard wheat:

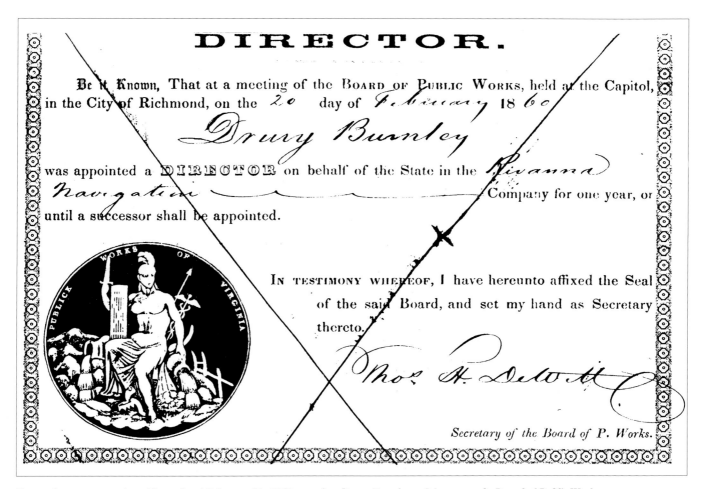

BOARD APPOINTMENT. *A certificate dated February 20, 1860, appoints Drury Burnley as Director on the Board of Public Works, representing the Rivanna Navigation Company.*

Flour from this grain did not mildew on the clipper ships that crossed the Equator bound for South America and the California gold fields. These years saw the building of new churches, beautiful homes, a new Court House inspired by plans drawn by Jefferson, new roads and bridges. However, by 1854, just a few years after the ambitious rebuilding of the Rivanna navigation, farmers and millers faced financial ruin because, according to most sources, the wheat crops failed

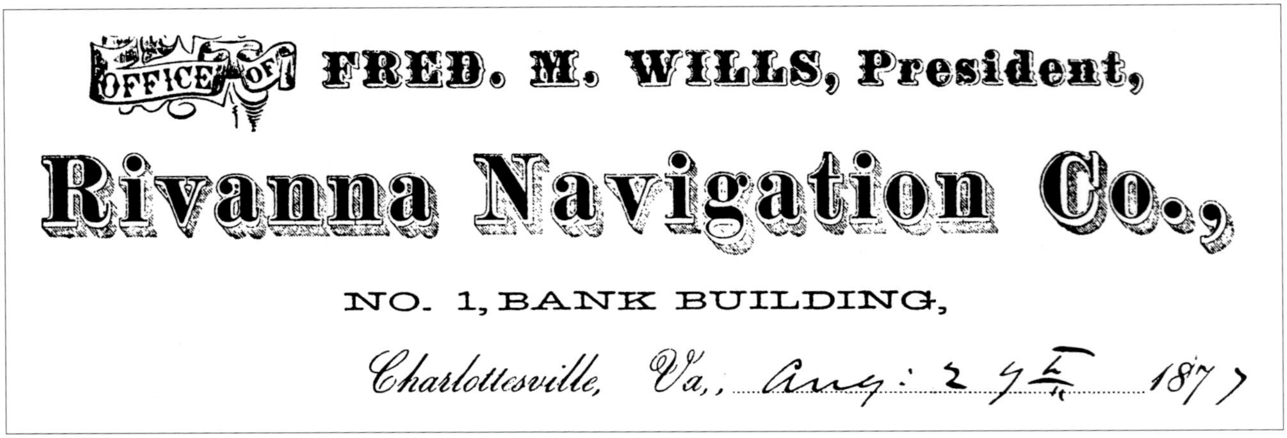

OFFICE OF FRED. M. WILLS, President,

Rivanna Navigation Co.,

NO. 1, BANK BUILDING,

Charlottesville, Va., Aug: 29th 1877

LETTERHEAD. *Fred M. Wills's stationery as president of the Rivanna Navigation Company, 1877.*

and grain from the Midwest began to flood the market. The producers did not recover before the Civil War began in 1861.

The Rivanna navigation survived the Civil War with no damage to the stone structures. The northern army attempted to destroy the massive stone aqueduct over the Rivanna at Columbia; Fluvanna (and the James River and Kanawha Company) were thankful the soldiers were unsuccessful. They burned bridges and destroyed boats, and it seems a wonder the soldiers left the dams and locks intact, but perhaps they carried no explosives. However, they raided and burned mills.

The worst enemies of the Rivanna navigation were floods. The great flood of 1870 damaged it severely. The company refused to give up, and in 1871 it made an effort to raise funds to improve at least the navigation to Charlottesville. Records for this period are fragmentary. Woods states that two dams were constructed in Albemarle, one above Milton, the other above Shadwell, but floods damaged them and they were abandoned. Work was also done at Pireus, Stump Island and Buck Island.

Green Peyton's map of Albemarle, published in 1875, notes locks at Shadwell, Milton and Stump Island, but an 1880 survey of dams in Albemarle lists Shadwell Dam as "broken" and Buck Island as "defunct."

STUMP ISLAND DAM, LOOKING UPSTREAM. The river is gradually washing away the bank, revealing a stone dam, with an abutment at left. If there was a lock here, it has not yet been uncovered.

PETE RUNGE

WARREN ANDERSON

"To be rented[:] A Mill seat, Near Charlottesville, Albemarle county, Virginia, at the head of the navigation of the Rivanna river, being the North branch of James river. [T]he water for the mill is taken out of the river about three quarters of a mile above the seat of the mill house . . . ."

Th: Jefferson

(1793)

7

THE RIVANNA'S VILLAGES

On the Rivanna, deeper water for transportation encouraged development, including more mills. The mills attracted shops—perhaps a cooper, blacksmith, and cobbler—a store, a cluster of houses and a post office, creating small mill villages in Albemarle and Fluvanna. Two of the largest communities, Charlottesville and Columbia, continued to grow after the navigation was no more, because of other commerce and institutions. Palmyra continued as a county seat, but most mill centers have been abandoned. Only the ruins of once proud buildings, and a few lovely old homes, remain as testaments to the past.

MILLS IN ALBEMARLE

All the water-powered mill structures are gone, now only a part of county history. Rio Mills was once the center of a thriving community. The builder, William Meriwether, sold the mill in 1835 to Nathaniel Burnley. Just beneath the covered bridge, a milldam turned water into a canal for the overshot waterwheel for this mill, which stood on a nearby creek bank.

Abraham Hildebrand became the owner in 1863. To escape the ravages of the Civil War, he had sold his mill in the Shenandoah Valley and crossed the mountains with two wagons loaded with wheat, to begin grinding corn and wheat and sawing lumber at Rio. Nearby was a blacksmith shop, cooper's shop and store. After Union General George Armstrong Custer burned the mill on February 29, 1864, Hildebrand rebuilt and continued to operate, though the freight batteaux no longer came that far up the Rivanna. The Hildebrand family ran the mill until 1925.

EARL C. LEAKE

MECHUMS RIVER MILL. In the Rivanna's vast watershed in Albemarle County, draining the eastern flanks of the Blue Ridge, each stream had at least one grain mill, such as Mechums River Mill, pictured c. 1940. On the North Fork there were, among others, Ferneyhough's (Burnt Mill) and Fry's (later Advance Mills), and on branches of the South Fork, Norris's, Ballard's, Brown's (on Doyles River), and Maupin's.

CHARLOTTESVILLE'S WOOLEN MILLS. The last textile mill on the river, near the mouth of Moore's Creek at the old Pireus site, closed in 1962.

Though the miller's cottage still stands, the other structures were destroyed for the South Fork Rivanna River Reservoir.

Power from the Rivanna dam at Pireus ran a succession of mills; a textile mill there closed and was followed by the Charlottesville Woolen Mills, which was chartered in 1868 and prospered for almost a century, making woolen cloth for military uniforms. Today the waterfall of the dam sings for its own amusement; the mill village with its small church has become just a part of the city of Charlottesville.

After Jefferson's death in 1826, the Magruder and Timberlake families purchased his mills, and followed in his footsteps with an ongoing debate with the navigation company. In 1845 the General Assembly passed an act allowing the owners and others to incorporate a stock company at Shadwell Mills, to be known as the Monticello Manufacturing Company. Union soldiers burned Jefferson's mills and they were not rebuilt. Today it is an important archeological site worth studying.

There are still lovely old homes near the bridge at Milton, but the commercial life died. A report of 1880 noted the Milton Dam was "used by Jno. C. Chewning or Snead Chewning," and Stump Island dam was "used by B. H. Magruder & Son for milling . . . ." Flanagan's Mill at Buck Island dam was burned by Federal troops, and it is uncertain that it was rebuilt. Ruins of it are still visible today. The river has claimed these sites for its own, welcoming the growth of sheltering trees.

IN FLUVANNA

The Richmond and Alleghany Railroad laid tracks on the towpath of the James River and Kanawha Canal in 1881. In Fluvanna, traffic on the Rivanna was heavy with crossties and supplies for the builders, but soon the boats were stopping at Columbia to transfer freight to the railroad. There followed almost two decades of some prosperity for the navigation and the mills. Even the small ports near Broken Island, Lane's and Flanagan's Landing were busy, and C. E. Jones built a store near his Carysbrook Mill. Just downstream where Carys Creek enters the Rivanna was East Point, with a store and a wharf, and in 1884 Cary Creek Post Office opened in William Anderson's store.

UNION MILLS

In central Fluvanna the Rivanna created commerce and villages. In 1890 Union Mills was flourishing. The large textile mill, the Union Factory, stood beside the early structures that housed the mechanisms for the grist mill, merchant mill

CHARLES P. JONES

REMAINS OF GRIST MILL AT UNION MILLS. Surrounded by other ruins near the banks of the Rivanna, the walls of the grist mill withstood the forces of nature better than most of the others. It was identified by timbers that held the "lewis" that lifted the upper grinding stone.

UNION FACTORY. Though gone today, in 1970 the basement walls were intact, and the building's chimney was still standing.

CHARLES M. WINKLER

GATE FROM A MILLRACE. At Union Mills, the race was used by batteaux as early as 1799. In the 1950s, the owner of Union Hall moved the stone of a guard gate from the millrace on the east side of the river to erect a unique entrance to his driveway on Route 616. A gate such as this protected the mills from floods; probably there was a pair of gates to let boats in and out of the race.

and sawmill, tended by two millwrights. Nearby stood the store and post office, the blacksmith shop, distillery, a tannery, a long barracks for the mill workers, a few dwellings and a small Methodist Church. There was one undertaker in the community. On the highland stood Cumber and Union Hall, impressive homes of the early owners of the mills, the Magruder and Timberlake families. Nearby was Oakland, the home of later owners, the Armstrong family.

It all began in 1792, when John Bowie Magruder moved from Bowie, Maryland, to the east bank of the Rivanna near

Adams Falls; by 1796 he secured permission from the county court to build a partial dam in the river. Two years later, he was ready to put a dam all the way across the river "from his canal for the purpose of working several mills." In 1807 he was required to put a batteau lock in his dam. One hundred and fifty years later, the owner of Union Hall moved the massive stones from a guard gate on the millrace to create a unique entrance to his driveway on Route 616.

In the 1880s the mills were among the most valuable properties in the county, but by 1890 they were in financial trouble. Exact documentation has not been found, but most sources state the fabric mill closed at the end of the nineteenth century and the grain mills closed soon after. Today the river environment has overtaken the area, and the ruins of the buildings are covered with greenery. If one sits on a log in the shade of riverside trees, he can imagine the hustle and bustle of boats and horses and wagons, men scurrying to and fro with shouts of command or bursts of laughter. But he will hear only bird song and water threshing through the broken dam.

BERNARDSBURG/CROFTON

There is no record of a mill on the river at the early dam, as there was always a mill on Boston Creek, a stream that entered the river just below the locks. This mill and the store near the upper lock both prospered because of the river navigation. The name of the settlement changed when a post office named Crofton opened in the store in 1897. The Martin King Ford upstream was aban-

BOSTON MILL. Located on Boston (or Adrians) Creek near the Crofton locks, most of this basement was destroyed in the building of the dam for Lake Monticello.

73

PALMYRA COVERED BRIDGE. First burned at the end of the Civil War, the bridge was rebuilt, then destroyed by flood in 1870 and 1877. It was rebuilt the last time by Capt. J.H. Anderson and C.C. Cocke. They erected it using 3,000 white oak pegs, boiled for a week to destroy insects.

doned and Chastain C. Cocke built one of his special river bridges for the county here. This bridge was later replaced by a steel overhead-truss one-lane bridge, which in turn yielded to a wide modern bridge that now carries Route 600 over the river.

The remains of the mill, store and miller's house near the locks were all destroyed by the development of Lake Monticello. The towpath and canal below Route 600 have been stirred from their long slumber as Lake residents reclaimed the area from overgrown wilderness. This section of towpath, canal and two locks below the highway have been placed on the state and national Registers of Historic Places.

CHARLES M. WINKLER

WHO WAS "RMC"? The General Assembly gave permission to the Reverend Walker Timberlake in 1828 to build the first covered bridge across the Rivanna at Palmyra. A stone mason dated the eastern pier: RMC – AU 2, 1828.

The towpath is now a lovely trail, and one can walk beside the old canal shaded by tall trees, enjoy the fragrance of spice bushes and watch for the pawpaw trees and their exotic fruit.

PALMYRA

When the Reverend Walker Timberlake and his brother John, Jr., built their mill on the Rivanna, they asked that a new road be built to the Courthouse that would pass the mill. Next Walker asked the General Assembly for permission to put a toll bridge across the river at their mill site. The covered bridge was completed in 1828, when the county seat was moved to a site above his mill, and Timberlake collected the tolls until the county purchased the bridge. The county seat adopted the name of the mills, Palmyra.

CENTENNIAL STAMP. The artist who drew this 1952 stamp said he used the portal of Palmyra's covered bridge (RIGHT) as his model.

GOOD-BYE TO THE COVERED BRIDGE. The Virginia Highway Department burned the sturdy bridge in 1930, claiming it might wash downstream and damage the new steel Pembroke Pettit Bridge. Fluvanna folk stood on the new bridge and watched the flames through tears.

A wooden bridge was covered to protect the timbers from the weather so they would not rot, and to keep the teams from bolting at the sight of the flowing water below.

Floods would carry this covered bridge downstream, where it would find anchorage in a sharp bend of the river just above Strange's batteau lock. Workmen would take the bridge apart, carefully numbering the timbers, haul it back upriver and rebuild it. After the 1850 dam was built downstream, the bridge was in the deep water of the millpond and much more vulnerable to floods. When there was no bridge, the county operated a ferry.

PALMYRA MILLS. Reverend Walker Timberlake and his brother John built their mill in 1813–14, using rock for the basement and first floor and brick for the upper stories. This is the rear view.

PALMYRA MILLS

When the Timberlakes dug a canal from their first dam to their mill site in 1813, they built a tall mill with a fireplace in the rock wall of the first floor, which also featured a Dutch door, hung in two sections so the upper half could be opened for air while the lower half kept out stray animals.

There is no sign here, or at other river mills, that an outside millwheel (overshot, undershot or breast) was ever used to power mills on the lower Rivanna, so it is believed that they were tub mills and later were converted to vertical turbines, which have been found at Palmyra and other sites. The dam broke after World War I.

CHARLES M. WINKLER

REMAINS OF PALMYRA MILLS. The walls survived torching by Union troops, and the interior was rebuilt. The brick walls of the upper stories were dismantled in the early 1930s for use in another building, but the rock walls stand, with metal remains of the mill machinery buried in the silt.

Like other mills on the river, this was a merchant mill, which bought grain and shipped the finished products down the river. They ground corn for cornmeal and wheat for flour and plaster (see Chapter 6) for the farmers.

In 1890 Palmyra had two mills, two hotels, five merchants, a saloon, two distillers, two coach and wagon builders, a physician, an undertaker and a tanner. The coming of the railroad in 1908 destroyed workshops adjacent to the mill on Water Street, and in 1930 U.S. Route 15 removed a warehouse and a big distillery. Today there are still foundations of a few buildings near the mill.

Plans for Fluvanna's Heritage Trail include this area, but gone are the sounds of the mill, the falling water, the creaking of cog wheels, the grating of grain elevators, the rattle of grain into hoppers and the rumble of the grinding stones.

COLUMBIA

Columbia, near the state arsenal at Point of Fork, became Fluvanna's first incorporated town and grew at the junction of two navigations. Until recent years it was always a busy place, and evidently Columbia did not suffer as much financially in the 1850s as the rest of the county because of nearby gold mines. The 1850 census stated that Commodore Fielding Stockton invested $25,000 in his gold mine.

BATTEAU LOCK AT COLUMBIA. Remains of the last batteau lock on the Rivanna before the James, near Columbia, just above the railroad bridge.

During the Civil War there was a naval installation near the town, and in 1868 a gazetteer listed 17 stores in the Columbia area. After 1881 the town had a railroad and a canal, and by 1890 boasted one mill, 12 merchants, one iron foundry, two insurance agents, two millers, two newspapers, a tailor, an undertaker, four physicians, as well as attorneys and a dentist. There were also two vineyards, the growers following in the steps of Jefferson, whose efforts led to vineyards near Monticello.

Columbia was a canal town, but floods have devastated most of the old homes of the families who watched the proud packet boats and the loaded freight boats on the canals. These places exist only in faded pictures and newspaper clippings.

RIVANNA MILLS

Union Mills, Crofton, Palmyra and Columbia all had post offices, as did Rivanna Mills, but the latter was not a village—it was the busiest commercial site on the Rivanna. The post office was named Stillmans for the men who ran the mills, store and shops.

In 1897 many roads converged into the Bryant Ford Road leading to the Rivanna Mills, and the laden wagons and bug-

RIVANNA MILLS. John Ashlin received permission from county justices to dam the Rivanna in 1809 and established a merchant mill and grist mill that he named Rivanna Mills. Under the subsequent ownership of Robert White Ashlin, the mills were operated by George Stillman and later by John Rison, a kinsman. The mills were also called Ashlin's Mills, Stillman's Mills, and Rison's Mills.

gies cut the roadbed ever deeper into the steep hillsides lead-ing to the mills. During the busy season the flour mill ran day and night. Through the fields or up the towpath of the Connexion Canal men came bestride a mule or a blooded mare, moving aside for the patient animals that pulled the wagons and laden boats.

Local wisdom decreed, "If you want to have fun, go to East Point; if you want to do business go to Rivanna Mills." And what a business center it was! John Ashlin first dammed

CHARLES P. JONES

REMAINS AT RIVANNA MILLS. These are remains of the flour mill; the wall on left encloses the mill yard. Virginia Canals and Navigations Society members have since removed the tree from the basement window.

the Rivanna in 1809 and established a merchant mill and grist mill. He asked the Stillman brothers to help young Robert White Ashlin run the diverse businesses.

Three men, Robert Ashlin and George and Samuel Stillman, lived at Rivanna Hall and ran the commercial complex that threaded its way into the homes and agricultural life of the county. Ashlin supervised the plantation, and he and the Stillman brothers did a brisk business with the men on the boats on the Rivanna. Samuel ran an unusually busy general store, and George ran the mills. George was in charge of the lock at the mills and the connection lock at Columbia, and served as a director of the Rivanna Navigation Company. At the mills he collected the tolls for the navigation, maintaining a port of embarkation and transportation for river traffic.

There were storage warehouses for lumber, bricks and tobacco. Meticulously kept account books for the flour and

RIVANNA MILLS DAM TODAY. The site of Rivanna Mills includes some of the most beautiful old stonework found in Virginia today. The "eye" in the dam is the forebay, which allowed water from a canal to enter the millrace. A wooden barrier was lowered down the face of the dam to close the forebay, and rested on a wooden sill (which still remains). To the left of this picture the stonework curves into the lock wall.

METAL COGWHEEL. This gear protrudes from the silt filling the flour mill at Rivanna Mills. We believe it connects to a buried turbine, which ran the mill machinery.

grist mills, store, blacksmith shop, and cooper's shop have survived; these list the names of Fluvanna folk written with beautiful Spencerian flourishes. At one time there was a cobbler's shop and a sawmill.

At Rivanna Mills is found some of the most beautiful stonework in Virginia. The eastern stone abutment for the dam is very long; the "eye" in the dam is the forebay that allowed water from an approach canal to enter the millrace. Local folk called this beautifully built opening "the forby." A wooden barrier was lowered down the face of the dam to close the forebay when the mills were not operating, the shutter resting on a big wooden sill below the forebay; the sill is still there. From the forebay the stone wall curved for the upper end of the lock.

ASHLIN FAMILY CEMETERY. *Inscribed on a marker (SEE ARROW): "In Memory of George Stillman. He was born in Machias, Me., Nov. 13, 1788. Moved to Richmond, Virginia in 1810, served in the War of 1812, settled in Fluvanna County in 1815, was a magistrate 30 years, and a member of the Legislature 13 years. Died June 28, 1868, honored for his moral worth and virtues. He was a son of Gen. George Stillman of the Continental Army of the Revolution." On the reverse: "Samuel Stillman. was born Dec. 4, 1795 and died Aug. 7, 1874. In connection with his brother George and Col. Robt. W. Ashlin, he conducted a mercantile business for more than 45 years at Rivanna Mills and retained the confidence and respect of all men."*

In the 20th century the mills were run by a kinsman, John Rison, so Rivanna Mills had successive local names: Ashlin's, Stillman's, and Rison's Mill.

FAMILY CEMETERY

The Ashlin family cemetery crowns a hill above the Rivanna, surrounded by a wall of old brick and guarded by boxwood, oak and cedar. Isolated by miles of timber, a stillness and calm hover here. In spring the blue of the wide-eyed periwinkle covering the graves joins the mournful hue of the redbud bloom in a symphony of subtle color. Here lie Robert White Ashlin, his wife and kin. The largest tombstone was erected by the Ashlin children for the Stillman brothers. A row of ancient cedars bordered the slave cemetery nearer the mills.

UPSTREAM, TOWARD THE PAST. Remains of a milldam, North Fork, Rivanna River.

PETE RUNGE

BETTY McGEHEE

"The late flood has swept all mills in our neighborhood. [A]bout one half of my mill dam is gone . . . . Wood's mill on the river has stood tolerably well. Macgruder's dam has stood, but the lock is gone, which interrupts our navigation . . . ."

Th. Jefferson

(1807)

8

VANISHING TOWPATHS: GOOD-BYE TO AN ERA

Wholesale abandonment of the canals in central Virginia has given the impression that they were unsuccessful. Construction cost was high, and there were maintenance problems, but water has always been the most economical means of freight transport. Canals were certainly a blessing to farmers, who could ship their wheat, corn, tobacco, lumber, firewood, whiskey and other produce to market on regularly scheduled boats and receive needed supplies in return.

With time, one of the problems with the Rivanna boat traffic was the lack of a town at its northern terminus to ensure a market and passengers at each end. The navigation did not go anywhere—except through the middle of Fluvanna, a small county. The company attempted to improve the line to Charlottesville to fulfill Jefferson's visions, but a special dilemma was posed by the mills at Milton and Shadwell: If the dams were raised to the necessary height, the water would "drown" the mill wheels upstream and thereby stop the mills.

The James River and Kanawha Canal had yielded to the railroad, but the Rivanna Navigation Company continued until 1908. Its continued operation was actually connected to the railroad. When the Richmond and Alleghany bought the James River Canal, they agreed to maintain navigation on the Rivanna Connexion Canal. The railroad's annual report for the year ending September 30, 1885, stated that, in order for the citizens

GIFT TO THE OLD STONE JAIL MUSEUM BY ASHLIN WYATT SMITH

RIVANNA HALL. Home to the extended Ashlin family and to the Stillman brothers, the house stood on the hill above the mills. It was taken down and the timbers, floor and millwork were transported to Colonial Williamsburg. Brick from the basement has been used in at least two Fluvanna homes. Rivanna Mills lock appears in the foreground at left; the rough stone wall of the boat basin is at right.

of Fluvanna "to derive any benefit therefrom, it has been necessary to keep up the remainder" of the navigation.

So, appealing to the court, the railroad "after many efforts, obtained control of the whole line, free from obligation, other than open it to navigation . . . and keep it in repair, not exceeding $700 per year. Under this arrangement $3,500 have been expended, and a regular line of boats owned and run by the citizens [are] now plying the navigation" for 25 miles to Union Mills. "The railroad revenue from business thus secured is considerably in excess of the promised expenditures, and an important increase may be looked for in the future."

The annual reports of the railroad give details of navigation repairs made in 1887 and 1888. The Chesapeake and Ohio bought the Richmond and Alleghany in 1889–90, and with great reluctance assumed the obligation for maintaining the navigation.

By 1905 the railroad was neglecting the Rivanna, and C. E. Jones of Carysbrook Plantation insisted that a survey of the navigation be made, including soundings in the Connexion Canal.

A Fluvanna attorney, A. J. Taylor, took the county's suit to Richmond in 1907. The Chesapeake and Ohio agreed to build a railroad for Fluvanna, but it did not follow the Rivanna River northward from Columbia. Called the Virginia Air Line Railroad, it branched from the James River line of the Chesapeake and Ohio near Bremo Bluff, crossed the Rivanna near Carysbrook and followed the river to Palmyra; from there the line turned north to meet the Washington line.

Because of the old agreement John Rison of Rivanna Mills sued the railroad, seeking better maintenance of his milldam. Finally the railroad bought the mills, assuming ownership in 1912. The mills ran no more. The brick walls were taken down and the brick used for an office building in Palmyra.

Boats on the Rivanna were very busy just before their disappearance, for they again carried crossties, rails and supplies for yet another railroad. A team of mules could pull a wagon loaded with 10 to 15 hand-hewn or sawed wooden crossties, but one man, the owner of a big boat, claimed that just one mule could pull a boat laden with 350 ties.

Then the days of river freight were gone. A lonely silence descended along the banks of the Rivanna.

By the middle of the twentieth century, the canals and towpaths were cloaked with trees and underbrush, and now some of the small stone towpath culverts have collapsed. One summer day we took a family of Ashlin descendants down the Bryant Ford Road to Rivanna Mills. A little two-year-old girl, appropriately named Ashlin, was at first frightened by the roar of the water as it crashed against the rocks of the broken dam, but we adults tried to imagine the fall of water when the 19-foot dam was standing. Little Ashlin had no thought for that, nor did she miss the rumble of machinery in the mills, nor the ringing of hammers in the shops. She did not wish to hear the horn of an approaching boat, nor the snorting and stamping of waiting teams. Little Ashlin forgot about being scared, stripped to the buff and waded into the shallow water in the shadow of the ruins of her ancestor's flour mill.

RIVANNA CONNEXION CANAL. This photograph dates from c. 1908, when the canal was abandoned.

WARREN ANDERSON

"The grounds contain about three hundred acres, washed at the foot for about a mile, by a river of the size of the Schuykill."

9

VESTIGES: MEMORIES AND DISCOVERIES

How vivid were the memories of the days of boats and mills! We were fortunate to tap into the recollections: so clear, so filled with details and nostalgia was this inherited memory, handed from one generation to the next. It was not that our elders "lived in the past," it was just that the past and present blended to make every day a deeper experience. The chain of memory has broken, however, and with the passing of that one last generation, the boats and mills have truly disappeared. Today's families are more mobile; the fireside and the porch are no longer the family centers for conversation—and the youngsters find and define their world through the eyes of *Sesame Street*, MTV and the Internet. No longer do children curl up in a chair, listening to the old folks tell the tales that were told to them, imagining themselves living in another time.

The mills were not modern contraptions, spotless and intricate and quite mysterious. When they ran, you saw how they worked. The water poured in, the turbine spun and the gears meshed. The grain rattled down the elevators and into the hopper, the stone millwheels turned, the miller bagged the meal or flour. His hat, shoulders and even his eyebrows were white with grain dust.

However, it was the mules and the boats that were remembered with the most nostalgia.

EARL C. LEAKE

COVERED BRIDGE AND DAM AT RIO MILLS. Earl C. Leake passed along a memory from his father. During a flood, Nathaniel Burnley was busy in his Hydraulic Mills when the high water washed the structure off its foundation and carried both mill and miller downstream under the covered bridge and over the dam at Rio Mills, on the South Fork of the Rivanna. The mill, floating like a boat, was caught by an obstruction and held long enough for folk to help Burnley out of his runaway millhouse; then the building continued downstream until it broke up.

91

Granville Anderson, the son of Captain J. H. Anderson, told how the Captain found he could not negotiate the lock at Palmyra during high water. The mules had been unhitched to cross the covered bridge and the crew was attempting to guide the boat into the canal leading to the lock. The men at the mill watched in horror as the strong current caught the boat, sure they would witness the death of all on board. However, Captain Anderson rode his boat, loaded with wheat, right over the milldam and landed upright to continue down the river. Another captain, when he found himself in a like situation, ordered his men to jump overboard. The boat hung on the top of the dam and broke up.

Granville Anderson also told how he and his father were caught by a bad summer storm while bringing in a load of wheat on the connection canal to Rivanna Mills. His description featured terrible winds and lashing rain; he portrayed a boat being swamped by high seas! They tried to cover the wheat to protect it, but were unsuccessful. When they reached the mills, they spread the wheat to dry in an upstairs area, hoping to save it, but it was ruined by mold, a great loss.

Julian Jones told a delightful story of mutiny on the towpath. A man or a boy called a "hoggee" always rode or walked behind the mules that pulled the freight boats. That day the hoggee found the orders shouted to him by the captain offensive; he stopped, unhitched the towline, and headed back along the towpath to home port with his mules—leaving the captain shouting to the empty air, his boat dead in the water! Mr. Jones also remembered that when his father's boat got stuck on a sandbar, they just helped a man called "Old Peter" over

CHARLES P. JONES

WATER-LEVEL BRIDGES. Chastain Cocke built three water-level bridges on the Rivanna for Fluvanna County, near Union Mills, at Crofton, and at Rivanna Mills. Rough rock piers and the iron bolts that held the bridge continue to create islands in the river at Crofton; at Rivanna Mills the sites of the piers are quite visible, as shown above, and bolts and a timber that anchored the bridge remain on the banks (below).

the side, and he was so strong he would lift the boat right off the bar.

Anyone living along the river early in the twentieth century knew Wilmer White's mule, Scott, "the kickin'est mule in seven counties," who pulled a load of lumber downriver in the morning and a load of supplies for the new railroad upstream that afternoon.

Late in the nineteenth century Chastain C. Cocke built three "water-level bridges" on the Rivanna: below Union Mills, at Crofton, and below the dam at Rivanna Mills for the old Bryant Ford Road. These bridges were only a few feet above the medium water flow. The floor of his bridges were built on a slant, the upstream side lower than the downstream, so that logs and flood debris just went up and over without damaging the bridge. In a newspaper article Cocke claimed his bridges were not washed away by floods as conventional bridges were.

RIVANNA EXCURSION. This photograph captured the 1895 Easter Monday outing described, with embellishments, in a local newspaper.

Miss Fannie Wilkerson gave a vivid account of crossing the water-level bridge at Rivanna Mills. As they came down the long hill to the river she could hear the terrifying roar of the water falling over the high dam, and as they approached the river she crouched down on the floor of the carriage. When they reached the bridge the coachman had to dismount and blindfold the horses so he could lead them across.

One elderly lady had cherished a picture and a newspaper clipping from c. 1895, telling how a large group of young people, well chaperoned, enjoyed an Easter Monday pleasure cruise on the Rivanna from Carysbrook to Columbia in an empty freight boat. The reporter wrote the account with his tongue lodged firmly in his cheek. They "glided along," moving smoothly down the pleasant stream, regaled by the delightful music of the Fork Union band.

. . . different things of interest to the tourists were point-ed out to us. First East Point, where Aunt Lavinia sits

and follows the apostolic calling so much praised by the Puritans. Then the splendid farm of Mr. Marion Wood, where watermelons attain the size of hogsheads, and sweet potato vines reach such a length as to span the river. Then Buzzard's Rock, an immense cliff where so many of the graceful birds whose name it bears rest their wearied pinions. Then Stillman's Mill where the biggest fish stories of the world originate.

Then lastly, Columbia, whose tranquillity is disturbed only by the shriek of the locomotive and the yells of an Easter party . . . .

The thing that puzzled us most was how to turn around. Everybody had a different suggestion to make, but we all finally decided to leave it to the mule, whose sagacity in boatology was equaled only by the size of his ears, or to our giant-statured and ebony-featured Captain, Pete . . . . He succeeded in turning the boat around, which was the principal thing at the time. After getting straight a delightful dinner was served that would rival the menu of the finest Atlantic steamers . . . .

PETE RUNGE

RARE FIND IN A RIVANNA BATTEAU. A clay hearth for cooking meals on board.

Young boys playing in the Rivanna found the remains of this boat just below the Carysbrook bridge some 40 years later. If it has not moved downriver, it is now covered by a sandbar; we must watch for it to reappear!

In 1994 the first remains of a batteau were found on the Rivanna near Milton, one of the most exciting discoveries made by members of the Virginia Canals and Navigations Society. Lyle Browning, past president of the Archaeological Society of Virginia, dated the boat's construction back to Jefferson's time, between 1800 and 1840. The nails were machine-cut, and we would like to think that, if Jefferson did not own the boat, at least the nails were made in the Monticello shop! Pieces of pottery found in the hull, hand-painted polychrome Pearlware, led the explorers to surmise that the boat sank by 1840.

In the stern of the boat was the hearth where the batteau-men had cooked their meals—a rare find. VC&NS members hoped to secure permission to excavate the whole length of the boat and see the name of the owner painted on the bow, but permission was denied, and the next flood destroyed the visible remains.

Summer droughts of 1998 and 1999 created such low water in the Rivanna that the Canals Society members were able to find the ruins of other boats. Upstream from the mouth of Buck Island Creek, Pete Runge and others found a batteau that dates back to 1771–1800. Its ribs were held to the king plank with handmade nails and wooden pegs; so far this is the oldest batteau found on the Rivanna.

Downstream they found another boat in remarkably good condition, 67 feet long and only six feet wide. It was a type not previously known or even suspected. The same size as a batteau, but built like a canal boat, with high straight sides and a rudder, it was clearly designed to be towed from a towpath. Was this type designed to navigate the upper reaches of the Rivanna toward Charlottesville, through the old narrow batteau locks, where the standard canal boats, 93 by 14½ feet, could not go? Future research may tell us more about this unusual boat.

The explorers next found a portion of a batteau in the bank near Crofton boat landing. Then they discovered the remains of two canal boats in the west bank of the river nearby. Those who found the boats hope that someday they will have permission and the means to remove and preserve a Rivanna boat.

The most romantic ruin found on the river has been a sunken steamboat. The ambitious undertaking of Chastain C.

STEAMBOAT. *This 1972 news photograph shows Linda Shifflett of Palmyra viewing a model of the Rivanna steamer. The model, made by Theodore Haxall from measurements taken after the steamboat was uncovered by flood-waters, is now in Richmond's Valentine Museum. The only steamboat to ply the Rivanna was built by Chastain C. Cocke of Greenwood Plantation, and was noted in the 1887 report of the Richmond and Alleghany Railroad: "A steamboat has been put on the river by private parties and is making regular trips." A report the next year said that the steamboat had been "making regular trips until stopped recently by low water. There is a prospect of another steamer . . . ." However, the Cocke steamboat sank within a few years, and there was never a second. Before Hurricane Agnes moved the wreck of the boat in 1972, local people had removed its stove and other artifacts, dug a section of paddlewheel out of the mud and retrieved the axle. Milo Blauvelt used the salvaged section to build a replica of the paddlewheels on the original shaft. The eye on the top of the stove still had grease on it; the whistle (from the collection of Garnett Bourne) bears the initials C.C.C., for Chastain C. Cocke. The paddle-wheels and stove are on display at the Old Stone Jail Museum in Palmyra.*

THE SUNKEN STEAMBOAT. A flood during Hurricane Agnes in 1972 carried even this wreck away. The wreck was found again, farther down the river, shortly before publication of this book.

Cocke, this was the only steamboat to ply the Rivanna. Steamboats were not favored for use on canals, for the wash from the paddle wheels destroyed the banks, and the engine took up valuable cargo space. On the Rivanna every mule-drawn boat wanted to race the steamboat! About 1890 the boat was tied up at the Palmyra lock and the steam engine taken off to be used to thresh wheat, when a flood washed the boat from its moorings, carried it downriver to the curve previously visited by the Palmyra covered bridge, and deposited it against the west bank. It became a curiosity for boys playing on the river.

Plans to save the wreck never succeeded, and great floods in 1969 and 1972 lifted it from the riverbed and carried it away. A section of a paddle wheel, the long iron axle for the wheels, and many items from the cabin of the boat are preserved by the Old Stone Jail Museum at Palmyra.

Of all the river lore recalled by the older generation, nothing seemed to match the memories of the whistle of that steamboat. As we listened to the words of these recollections, heard the wistful note in our older friends' voices and saw the faraway look in their eyes, it seemed we could just hear the echoes of that piercing call, floating above the river.

OVERTON MCGEHEE

ALONG THE RIVANNA CONNEXION CANAL. "My River that rumbles o'er the remains of the past. My River . . . unlimited and vast." — lines from a poem by Doris Edmund McGehee, at age 12

97

OVERTON McGEHEE

"I have seen a leg of the rainbow plunge down on the river running through that valley."

Th: Jefferson

[To the Rev. J. Madison, describing the Rivanna's valley, below Monticello]

10

THE FUTURE OF AN AMERICAN TREASURE

The people who live in its vicinity are becoming aware that the Rivanna River is indeed their treasure. In our first efforts to secure recognition and preservation, the river was designated the first Scenic River in the State of Virginia, a 1974 honor conferred by the Legislature. This designation applied to the Rivanna in Fluvanna County; it was later extended up to the Woolen Mills dam in Albemarle.

Years of work have led to the formation of the Scenic River Advisory Board, and other organizations have become busy working on many approaches to preservation of this stream that lies at the heart of our counties; these include the Virginia Canals and Navigations Society, the Rivanna Conservation Society, the Fluvanna Historical Society, the Heritage Trail Foundation in Fluvanna, and the Rivanna Trails Foundation in Charlottesville. Through the years several studies of the Rivanna have been carried out by the Department of Landscape Architecture of the University of Virginia.

Now, through the efforts of the Thomas Jefferson Regional Planning District Commission, the Rivanna has been recognized again—a new designation by the National Trust for Historic Preservation: the Rivanna has been named an American Treasure, the only river so designated. It was recognized by the Save American Treasures program, a public–private partnership of the White House Millennium Council and the National Trust for Historic Preservation. The Rivanna thus joins the company of the Star-Spangled Banner, the Washington Monument and Fort McHenry.

But our treasure is in trouble. With more trees and pastureland in the watershed instead of row crops, the river does

POINT OF FORK. Here the Rivanna (RIGHT) flows into the James.

not run red with eroded soil as it once did, except when there is a construction site upstream. But we have so much more paved area near the river, that when rainfall is heavy, it raises the flow dramatically—and only temporarily, making the annual flow data give a false impression of the daily flow.

The river has a vast watershed, as any map will prove. However, in the summer, especially during a drought, the reservoirs above Charlottesville and the subdivisions near the river have cut the flow in Fluvanna so that we do not have enough water to flush the effluent downstream. At times the Department of Environmental Quality has noted that the river below the sewage treatment plants is polluted. The Rivanna Conservation Society tests the river water regularly, following the monitoring protocol of the Izaak Walton League, to count the number of healthy, pollution-sensitive organisms. But we need more monitoring, and constant vigilance.

We also need a study of projected water consumption, based on the rate of growth of subdivisions that will need water from the Rivanna. The population of Charlottesville and of the two counties is growing fast, as are Glenmore, Lake Monticello and other subdivisions being developed around Lake Monticello, which expect the water system of the Lake to furnish them water—water from the Rivanna. In addition, as of this writing, at least one power plant has been approved by Fluvanna County, which will take its water from the Rivanna.

The city of Charlottesville is exploring the possibility of yet another reservoir, to be built on Buck Mountain. If they build such a structure, shouldn't they plan to have enough water impounded from winter rains to allow them to release water during a drought to help the river flow? We need to avoid recreating the situation long seen on the Moormans River, a Rivanna tributary and another of our Scenic Rivers, which in summer ceases to flow below the Sugar Hollow reservoir.

We have studied the Rivanna River since 1960. Our plea is that we work together to save the historic sites on its banks, and to save the Rivanna itself—Mr. Jefferson's river, our navigation to history, our Stream of Pleasure.

TO JOIN:

The Fluvanna Historical Society
P.O. Box 8, Palmyra, VA 22963

The Rivanna Conservation Society
P.O. Box 141, Palmyra, VA 22963

The Virginia Canals and
Navigations Society
6826 Rosemont Drive
McLean, VA 22101

NOTES

Some sections of the first half of this book are based on the research of William E. Trout, III, published in a booklet, *The Rivanna Scenic River Atlas*. In this publication of the Virginia Canals and Navigations Society may be found more technical details of the founding and operation of the Rivanna Navigation Company, remains found today, and copious footnotes. Send $5 plus $2 postage to VC&NS Sales, 4066 Turnpike Rd., Lexington, VA 24450. Internet addresses: www.organizations.rockbridge.net/canal and www.batteau.org.

Abbreviations in the following notes: BPW, Board of Public Works; UVA, University of Virginia; LVA, Library of Virginia; VC&NS, Virginia Canals and Navigations Society; OSJM, Old Stone Jail Museum Archives; FCHS, Fluvanna County Historical Society.

INTRODUCTION

page 3: Mike W. Edwards, "Architect of Freedom: Thomas Jefferson," *National Geographic Society*, 149 (2), 231. Quoted by permission.

page 3: "The Scotchbroom that he planted . . . ." Peter Hatch, Monticello's director of gardens and grounds, verified that Jefferson grew Scotchbroom there. See also Merrill D. Peterson, quoted in *Garden and Farm Book*, Robert C. Baron, ed. (Golden, Colo.: Fulcrum, 1987), 11.

page 4: ". . . placed first on the list his efforts to make the Rivanna River navigable . . ." Dumas Malone, *Jefferson, the Virginian* (New York: Little, Brown, 1948), 115–116; and Barbara McEwan, *Thomas Jefferson: Farmer* (McFarland), 104.

page 6: ". . . said to have described as his 'sea view.'" When we were young and taken to Monticello, the guides always introduced us to Jefferson's "sea view." Researchers at Monticello tell us that this is an oral tradition that refuses to die.

page 6: "work house of nature." Jefferson in a letter to Maria Cosway, Paris, Oct. 12, 1786. Courtesy of Gaye Wilson, Researcher, Thomas Jefferson Memorial Foundation. B.10.447 ("Head and Heart Letter").

CHAPTER 1

page 10: "I see that the petition of Ashlin . . . " Edwin Morris Betts, ed., *Thomas Jefferson's Farm Book with Commentary and Relevant Extracts From Other Writings*, University Press of Virginia, 1976, 408. Letters in Library of Congress.

page 11: Betts, *Farm Book*, 408.

pages 11–12: "In 1763 (I was then not quite of age) . . . " J. P. Boyd, ed., "Notes on the several acts of assembly for clearing the Rivanna River," *The Papers Of Thomas Jefferson*, Princeton University Press, 1950, V. 1, 88. Quoted by permission. George and Roger Thompson were the sons of one of the first justices of Albemarle, Joseph Thompson, who lived above the Rivanna at the place now known as Palmyra, on a plantation later named Solitude.

page 12: Jefferson had to send goods down by wagon. Betts, *Farm Book*, 385, 387, 391.

page 12: ". . . transferred to 'regular river craft' . . . " E. M. Betts, ed., *Thomas Jefferson's Garden Book*, American Philosophical Society, 1944, 315.

pages 12–13: Invention of the Reverend Robert Rose. Ralph E. Fall, *The Diary of Robert Rose*, McClure Press, 1977, 251.

page 13: Origins of the James River batteau. *The Tiller*, Vol. 6, No. 2, Virginia Canals and Navigations Society [VC&NS], August 1985, 11.

page 14: William C. Bugg registration. Receipt in the Fluvanna County Miscellaneous Records, Fluvanna Circuit Court, 1792. Cited in Ellen Miyagawa, "James River and Kanawha Canal in Fluvanna," *The Bulletin of the Fluvanna County Historical Society* [*Bulletin*, FCHS], No. 33, 1982.

pages 14–15: Continued use of canoes. T. J. Wertenbaker, "The Rivanna," *The Magazine of Albemarle History*, XIV, 1954–55, 3. Quoted by permission.

page 15: 1804 flood. Betts, *Garden Book*, 315–316.

page 16: "The river is regularly boatable . . ." Robert C. Baron, *Thomas Jefferson, The Garden and Farm Books*, 1987, Fulcrum Publishing, Golden, Colo., 91.

page 16: Drought. Betts, *Farm Book*, 407.

page 16: Rivanna Warehouse. Hening's *The Statutes at Large*, Vol. 12, 66.

page 16: Milton as port of Albemarle. Edgar Woods, *Albemarle County in Virginia*, Charlottesville, Va., 1901, 57–58.

page 16: Henderson's Warehouse. Hening, *The Statutes at Large*, Vol. 13, 42, 87.

pages 16–17: Nicolas's Warehouse. John W. Knapp and Tyson van Auken, "Historical Survey of Navigation on the Rivanna River, Virginia," unpublished manuscript, Norfolk District, Corps of Engineers, c. 1982; copy in library of Virginia Military Institute, 10. Also John Hammond Moore, *Albemarle, Jefferson's County, 1727–1976*, The University Press of Virginia, 1976, 32.

page 17: Bernardsburg. Shepherd's *The Statutes at Large*. Vol. 2, 31, 355.

CHAPTER 2

page 18: "The navigation of the Rivanna . . . . " Betts, *Farm Book*, 387.

page 19: Rivanna Company incorporation and officers and 1814 General Assembly authorization: A report of commissioners viewing the works on the Rivanna. Fluvanna County Circuit Court deeds, Book 7, 30 (1815),

31, 35, (1817); Crozet's Field Notes, Rivanna Navigation, 1826, Book II, LVA.

page 19: Sluices and wing dams to Martin's Mill. 11th BPW report, 1826, 73.

pages 19, 21: Tulloch's and Martin's mills. Acts of Assembly, 1819–20, 38. The act extending the navigation from Martin's up to Tulloch's mill notes that the petitioners "have opened the said river between the said mills." The act required a lock in Martin's dam.

page 21: Martin's action. Albemarle County Legislative Petitions, December 3, 1845. LVA. No wing dams or other signs of navigation have yet been found above Martin's Mill; the "opening" could have been only the clearing of downed trees.

page 21: List of locks. 4th BPW Report, Supplement for 1818 (1819), 49.

page 21: Pireus. Wertenbaker, "The Rivanna." Moore's Creek should not be confused with Moore's (sometimes spelled Moors) Ford which was two miles upstream at the present U.S. 250 bridge (Free Bridge).

page 21: Tolls. Fluvanna County Circuit Court deeds, Book 7, 1817, 31.

CHAPTER 3

page 22: "I am ready to cut my dam . . . . " Betts, *Farm Book*.

page 23: Canal du Midi. W. E. Trout, III, "Avec Thomas Jefferson sur le Canal du Midi," *American Canals*, Vol. 30, August 1979, 5.

page 23: Two connected locks. The back of a letter to Jefferson, about Tarleton's "ravages" during the American Revolution, dated April 24, 1788: Jefferson Papers, Library of Congress, Reel 9.

page 23: Latrobe drawing of drydock scheme. Darwin H. Stapleton, ed., *The Engineering Drawings of Benjamin Henry Latrobe* (Charlottesville, Va.: University Press of Virginia, 1980), 9–11, 120; Edwin T. Martin, *Thomas Jefferson, Scientist*, (New York: H. Schuman, 1952, 74–77.

pages 23–24: Proposed military canal. A. A. Lipscomb and A. E. Berg, eds., *The Writings of Thomas Jefferson*, Washington, D.C., 1903, Vol. 13, 232–236. See also William E. Trout, III, *The Great Dismal Atlas*, VC&NS 1998, 137.

page 24: Jefferson built on the same site. Betts, *Farm Book*, 387.

page 24: . . . blasted out of solid rock. Ibid., 343, 386–393; also "The Shadwell Mill Complex: Jefferson's Manufacturing, Toll Mill and Canal," by Amy Elizabeth Bennett, Master of Landscape Architecture thesis, UVA, 93 pp., May 1981.

page 24: Offer to provide a batteau. Betts, *Farm Book*, 378.

page 24: Widening of the canal. Jefferson planned to make the original canal 16 feet wide at the bottom in 1792 (Betts, *Farm Book*, 347). After its enlargement for batteaux it was 9 feet wide (whether at the surface or bottom is not stated). James E. Bear, Jr., *Jefferson at Monticello*, (Charlottesville, Va.: University Press of Virginia, 1967), 64.

pages 24–25: Letter to directors. As repeated, with some variation, in an 1811 letter to James Monroe (Betts, *Farm Book*, 382–383).

page 25: Locks ruined. Betts, *Farm Book*, 404.

page 25: Jefferson's map. Dumas Malone, *The Sage of Monticello* (Boston: Little, Brown, 1981), 39. The map and letter are in Betts, *Farm Book*, 386–393.

page 25: Architectural drawing of connected locks. Measurements, dated May 11, 1817, are with Jefferson's drawings, Nichols #476 (Kimball #169s), in the Massachusetts Historical Society. Copies are in the Alderman Library at UVA.

CHAPTER 4

page 26: ". . . we cannot get mills built." Betts, *Farm Book*.

page 27: New company secured a charter from the state. *Acts of Assembly* 1826–27, 58–61. The original 1827 list of subscribers (stockholders) is in Albemarle County Deed Book 27. (Woods, *Albemarle*, 84). The Minute Book of the company, 1828 to 1851, is in the Alderman Library, UVA.

page 27: The state invested in the company. 16th BPW Report, 1831, 488.

page 27: Company presidents. BPW Reports, 1848–1851.

pages 27–28: Crozet's conclusion. 11th BPW Report, 1826, 73. Crozet's field notes are in BPW Field Notes, Rivanna Navigation, Box 210, VSL. The resulting map has been lost and may no longer exist.

page 28: Primacy of navigation over mill rights. Fluvanna County Circuit Court deeds, Book 17, 1854, 46. Albemarle Circuit Court deeds, Book 68, 1873, 283. Knapp and Van Auken, 11.

page 28: Stillman's paper. Archives, OSJM, FCHS.

page 29: Responsibility for maintenance of locks. 18th BPW Report, 1833, 189; 25th BPW Report, 1840, 409.

page 29: Wood's Mill lock and dam. 17th BPW Report, 1832, 55–56.

page 29: Total number of locks. 22nd BPW Report, 266, 1837.

page 29: Meriwether at New Bridge. Woods, *Albemarle*, 73.

page 29: New Bridge, 1836. 23rd BPW Report, 409, 1838.

page 30: Rebuilding of Rio Mills. Information supplied by the great-grandson of Abraham Hildebrand, Earl C. Leake (who successfully campaigned to have a marker erected in 1991 to commemorate the Civil War Battle of Rio Mill).

pages 30–31: Broad Mossing Ford. 23rd BPW Report, 1838, 409. The island existed in the time of Claudius Crozet, for it is shown on his 1826 survey. Woods, *Albemarle*, 85, says there were two locks at Broad Mossing, but the records do not support this.

page 32: Crozet construction suggestion. 18th BPW Report, 1833, 189.

page 32: Crofton lock. Lyle E. Browning, "Crofton Lock," *Quarterly Bulletin, Archeological Society of Virginia*, Vol. 35 (No. 3, March 1981), 166–176.

page 32: Craven's report. Albemarle County petition to the Legislature, December 15, 1823, LVA.

page 35: Mill owners replied. Ibid, January 10, 1824.

CHAPTER 5

page 36: ". . . I must observe that I hold the lands . . . ." Betts, *Farm Book*, 377.

page 37: James River and Kanawha Canal in 1840. Boyd

M. Coyner, Jr., *John Hartwell Cocke of Bremo: Agriculture and Slavery in the Ante-Bellum South*, UVA, 1961, 262. Cocke was quite active in canal affairs.

page 37: Locks on the new canal. 23rd BPW Report, 1838, 410.

page 39: Sleeping arrangements. *Tiller*, VC&NS, Vol. 11, Issue 2, 7, 8, 9; Vol. 12, Issue 3, 11, 13; Vol. 15, Issue 3, 10, and other issues.

page 39: Specific record of a packet boat. Archives, OSJM, Weather Diary of Samuel Stillman, included in "Old Mills in Fluvanna," *Bulletin*, FCHS, No. 10–11, 1970. Minnie Lee McGehee, 30.

page 39: Petitions concerning improvements. Albemarle Petitions to General Assembly, Jan., 1847, LVA.

page 39: Investment in navigation, and the need to compete with railroads. Moore, *Albemarle*, 188.

pages 39–40: Plans of the James River and Kanawha Company. 37th BPW Report, 1852, 553.

page 40: The exact location of Thrift's Ford has not been pinned down. The Company's minute book entry for April 14, 1829 puts it 3¼ miles above the gut just below Union Mills, Minute Book of Rivanna Navigation Company, 1828–1851, Alderman Library, UVA, #7364. Most agree Thrift's Ford is about ½ mile above the Fluvanna County line.

page 40: "50 tons burden." Moore, *Albemarle*, 188.

page 40: Couty's reputation. 37th BPW Report, 1852, 553. John Couty also built many of the locks on the Rappahannock Navigation. According to local information he is buried near old Bernardsburg, but across the river at Spring Hill.

page 41: Lock gate construction. Remains of lock gates found by the authors in the Rivanna, one in 1968 and one in 1988, and studies of other lock gates.

page 45: Always something new to discover. These observations and the following descriptions are based on observations of the authors of dams and locks on the Rivanna and those examined on other rivers. Also the reports of the James River and Kanawha Canal engineers who surveyed the Rivanna: "Improvements of the Rivanna River for Navigation by Towboats," 1842, LVA,

TC/435/R6/W9. The final construction of the locks and dams did not follow those plans. Copies of 55 plats drawn by Couty for the navigation from Columbia to Palmyra are in LVA and the Clerk's Office of Fluvanna County. The original survey plats, beautifully drawn and colored, were stolen from the Fluvanna Office in recent years.

page 51: Palmyra was the Roman name for ancient Tadmor, Bible. Family tradition holds that Rev. W. Timberlake chose this name.

page 51: Location of dam at Palmyra. Court Orders, Fluvanna Justices, 1813: Clerk's Office.

page 51: 1850 rebuilding at Palmyra. Deed Book 16, 318–319; Deed Book 17, 14, 1854, Fluvanna.

page 55: Flooding caused by Rivanna Mills dam. Rison vs. Chesapeake & Ohio, Archives, OSJM.

CHAPTER 6

page 62: ". . . I am sorry it is not in my power . . . ." Betts, *Farm Book*, 374.

page 63: Company report of 1848. 33rd BPW Report, 1848, 460.

page 63: Flanagan's Landing. WPA papers, Archives, OSJM.

page 63: Investment, 1851–1857. Moore, *Albemarle*, 187.

page 63: Navigation to Shadwell Mills. 29th BPW Report, 1844, 288; Acts of Assembly, 1844/45, 111.

page 64: Names of freight boats. Archives, OSJM; *The Tiller*, VC&NS, Vol. 11 (No. 1), 13 and Vol. 12 (No. 3), 8, W. E. Trout.

pages 65–66: Financial troubles, 1854–1861. Archives, OSJM; *Bulletin* No. 35, FCHS, David Bearr.

page 66: ". . . thankful the soldiers were unsuccessful." *Edward Lorraine Diaries and Papers, 1841–1867*, MSS1/L8935/a, Virginia Historical Society.

pages 66–67: 1871 fund-raising. 46th BPW Report, 1871, 142. In 1860 Edward Lorraine, Chief Engineer of the James River and Kanawha Canal, received permission from the Board of Directors to take charge of the unfinished portion of the Rivanna Navigation (Board of Directors Minutes James River and Kanawha Canal, March, 1860), but apparently nothing was done because of the Civil War. Lorraine died in 1872.

page 67: Dams and other work after 1871. Woods, *Albemarle County*, 85; Trout, *Rivanna Scenic River Atlas*, 30, VC&NS.

page 67: 1880 survey of dams. Board of Public Works, Box 52, under "fish ladders," VSL.

CHAPTER 7

page 68: "To be rented . . . ." Betts, *Farm Book*, 350.

page 70: ". . . other structures were destroyed for the South Fork Rivanna Reservoir." From information supplied by the great-grandson of Abraham Hildebrand, Earl C. Leake.

page 70: History of Charlottesville Woolen Mills. *Magazine of Albemarle County History*, Vol. 53, 1995.

page 71: Monticello Manufacturing Company. Acts of the Assembly, 1844/45, 111.

page 71: Report on the uses of Milton and Stump Island dams. Wertenbaker, "The Rivanna," 5.

page 71: Flanagan's Mill burned. WPA Records, Albemarle Co., Flanagan's Mill; VSL.

page 71: Freight transfer to the railroad at Columbia. Noel Harrison, "Years With the Air Line," FCHS, *Bulletin* No. 37.

page 71: Stores and post office at Carysbrook. Minnie Lee McGehee, "Post Offices of Fluvanna," FCHS, *Bulletin* No. 15.

pages 71–72: Union Mills community. Minnie Lee McGehee, ed., "Statistics," FCHS, *Bulletin* No. 9.

page 72: Cumber and Oakland still survive, although many changes and additions have been made. The Methodist Church was moved from the mill village to its present site on Rt. 616.

page 73: Mill closings at Union Mills. DB 2503, 39; oral tradition. For more on mills in Fluvanna see Minnie Lee McGehee, FCHS, *Bulletin* Nos. 10–11.

page 77: Bridge and ferry at Palmyra. *Midland Virginian*, OSJM.

page 80: Columbia account books. Account Books, Archives, OSJM.

CHAPTER 8

page 86: "The late flood has swept . . . ." Betts, *Farm Book*, 367.

page 87: Dilemma between dams and mills at Milton and Shadwell. BPW, Box 210, Rivanna Navigation correspondence, May 12, 1854, VSL.

page 88: Soundings in Connexion Canal. Conversations with Julian Jones.

page 88: Virginia Air Line Railroad. Noel Harrison, *Bulletin* No. 37, FCHS.

page 88: Railroad purchase of Rivanna Mills. Deed Book 31, Fluvanna County, 295.

page 88: Various claims of mules' pulling abilities. Conversation with W. W. White, see Minnie Lee McGehee, FCHS, Bulletin No. 5.

CHAPTER 9

page 90: "The grounds contain . . . ." Baron, *Thomas Jefferson, The Garden and Farm Books*.

pages 92–93: Accounts of mishaps at the lock at Palmyra. Conversation with W. W. White, see Minnie Lee McGehee, FCHS, *Bulletin* No. 5.

page 93: Wilmer White's mule. Conversation with W. W. White, see Minnie Lee McGehee, FCHS, *Bulletin* No. 5.

pages 93–94: Report on Easter Monday cruise. *Midland Virginian*, OSJM.

page 95: Discoveries in 1998–99. See issues of *The Tiller* from these years.

pages 95–96: Sunken steamboat. Conversations and picture-taking with Lyle Browning, State Archeologist, by W. E. Trout and Peter Runge.

INDEX

Note: Page numbers in italics refer to photographs and other illustrations, as well as captions.

A

Adams Falls 73
Adrians Creek (*see* Boston Creek)
Advance Mills (*see* Fry's)
Albemarle County 1, 4, *5*, 6, 11, 14, 37, 39, 63, 66, 67, 99; mills 69–71
Albemarle County Historical Society 1; library 1
Anderson, Captain J.H. *74*, 92
Anderson, Granville 92
Anderson, William 64, 71
Archaeological Society of Virginia 94
Armstrong family 72
Ashlin family *87*; cemetery *84*, 85
Ashlin, John 10, 21, 81
Ashlin, Robert White *81*, 82, *84*

B

Ballard's Mill *69*
Ballenger Creek 7
Barksdale's Mill 19
batteau *Fluvanna 33*
batteaux 1, 6; "invented" by Benjamin and Anthony Rucker 13; and James River 13; clay hearth found *94*, 95; description 13; initial launch witnessed by Thomas Jefferson 13; locks for, description 14; registration of 14; remains found *94*, 95; spelling 1
Bernard, Allen 17
Bernardsburg 17, 29, 32, 40, 73; locks 41
Blauvelt, Milo 95
Boston Creek (Adrians Creek) 7, 73
Boston Mill *73*
Bourne, Garnett 95
Braham, Nimrod 19
Bremo Bluff 88
Broad Mossing Ford 29, 30
Broken Island (*see also* Pettit's Island) 29, 40, 43, 71; Lane's 63, 71; lockkeeper's house *49*; locks 48–50, 63
Brown's Mill 69
Browning, Lyle 94
Bryan, John Randolph 27, *53*

Bryant Ford Road *56*, 89, 93; culvert *58*
Buck Island 67; dam 67
Buck Island Creek 6, 11, 95
Buck Mountain 100
Buck Mountain Creek 4
Bugg, William C. 14
Burke Creek 7
Burnley, Drury *65*
Burnley, Nathaniel 69, *91*
Buzzard's Rock 55
Burnt Mill (*see* Ferneyhough's)
Byrd Creek 12

C

Campbell's Mill 21, 28
canal boats 1, 6; locks and dams for 37–61
Canal du Midi 23
canals 23; building of 37; costs and benefits 87; Jefferson's interest in 23–24; relationship to batteaux 37
canoes 1, 11, *12*, 14–15; and Rev. Robert Rose 12–13; development of 12–13
Cary Creek Post Office 71
Carys Creek 7, 71
Carysbrook Mill *53*, *54*, 71
Carysbrook Plantation 27, 29, 32, 39, 53, 88; dam *53*; dam and lock 43–45; lock *54*
Castle Hill 11
Charlottesville 4, 6, 14, 19, 39, 69, 87, 95; as "Athens of the South" 21; reservoirs *29*, 70, 100
Charlottesville Turnpike 29
Charlottesville-Albemarle Railway *20*
Chesapeake & Ohio Railroad *38*, *50*, 88
Childress, Benjamin F. 64
Civil War 66, 69, 80
Clark, James 27
Cocke, Chastain C. 27, 28, 74, *92*, 93, 95
Cocke, John H. 27
Coleman's Dam *50*
Columbia 3, 6, 14, 16, 18, 19, 21, 29, 37, 40, 45, 66, 69, 71, 80, 88; batteau lock 80; gold mines 80; junction lock 45, 59,

60; St. Andrews Street 59
Couty, John 40–41, 45, *56*, 59, *60*
Craven, John H. 32
crib dams 31; 1813 dam at Palmyra 31; 1850 dam at Palmyra 31; method of construction 31
crib fords 30–31
Crofton 32, 45, 73, 80, *92*, 93, 95; batteau lock *33*; canal locks 46–48
Crozet, Claudius 21, 29, 32; survey of the Rivanna 27–28
Cumber 72
Cunningham Creek 7
Custer, George Armstrong 69

D

Dismal Swamp Canal 37
Divers, George 19
Dog Creek 7, 57
Dog Point 43
Dollins Creek 4
Doyles River 69

E

East Point 71, 81
Edwards, Mike W. 3

F

fall line 3
Ferneyhough's (Burnt Mill) 69
Flanagan's Landing 63, 71
Flanagan's Mill 71; burned by Union troops 71
Flood of 1771 13, 15, 24
Flood of 1870 66
Flood of 1929 *29*
Fluvanna County 1, 3, 6, 8, *17*, 27, 28, *34*, 37, 39, *58*, 63, 87, 99; boatbuilders 64; commerce with South America and California 65; cultivation of wheat 64–65; Heritage Trail 79; mills 71–85
Fluvanna County Historical Society 1, 99, 100
Free Bridge *31*
Fry's (Advance Mills) 69

G

Gazeteer of Virginia 35
Glenmore 100
Goochland County 12
Greene County 4

Greenwood Plantation *95*
Gum Creek 7, 57

H

Haxall, Theodore 95
Henderson's Warehouse 16
Heritage Trail Foundation 99
Hildebrand family 30, 69
Hildebrand, Abraham Louis 30, 69
Hughes, John G. 29
Hurricane Agnes 95, *96*
Hydraulic Mills 19, 29, *91*; bridge *29*
Hydraulic Road 29

I

Izaak Walton League 100

J

James River 3, 6, *17*, 19, 21, 37, *50*, 99; as the Fluvanna River, west of Columbia 3
James River and Kanawha Canal 29, 37–38, 45, *60*, 87; aqueduct 29, 37, *38*, 66; effect on Rivanna navigation 39; packet boats on 38–39
James River and Kanawha Company 45, 55, 59, *64*, 66
Jamestown *17*
Jefferson, Thomas 2, 3–4, 6, 10, 11–16, 18, 22, 26, 36, 61, 62, 65, 68, 80, 86, 87, 90, 94, 98; and the Rivanna Company 24–25; death 27, 70; design for connected locks 23; design for locks at Milton 25; design for Navy Yard lock 23; interest in Canal du Midi 23; map of Shadwell 25; mills and canals at Shadwell 24–25; proposed military canal 23–24
Jones, C.E. 71, 88
Jones, Julian 92
Jones, William 64
junction lock 45, 59, *60*

K

Kelly, John 19

L

Lake Monticello 17, 46, *73*, 74, 100
Latrobe, Benjamin Henry 23

Leake, Earl C. *91*
Long Island Creek 7
Lynchburg 37

M

Macon, Colonel Thomas 27
Madison, Rev. J. 98
Magruder family *35*, *63*, *70*, *72*
Magruder, John Bowie 21, 72
Manakin's Ferry 39
Martin King Ford 73
Martin's Mill 19, 21
Martin, George 21
Martin, Joseph 35
mason's marks *51*
Maupin's Mill *69*
Maury River (North River) 37
McGehee, Doris Edmund 97
Mechums River 4
Mechums River Mill *69*
Mechunk Creek 6, 52
Meriwether, William H. 19, 27, 29, 69
milldams 21; improvements 27; in Albemarle County 21; in Fluvanna County 21
mills; conflict with navigation rights of boats 28
Milton 15, *15*, 16, 17, 18, 19, 29, 32, 66, 67, 71, 87; as the Port of Albemarle 16; bridge 15
Milton Falls 12, 18, 25
Minor, Dabney 19
Monacan nation *17*
Monticello 3, 4, 6, 23, 24
Monticello Manufacturing Company 71
Moore's Creek 6, 21, 29
Moormans River 4, 100
Mt. Misory Creek 7

N

National Trust for Historic Preservation 99
New Bridge 29
Nicolas's Warehouse 16
Noel family 51
Norris's Mill *69*

O

Oak Hill Plantation (*see also* Strange's Farm) 53, *54*
Oakland 72
Old Stone Jail Museum 1, *95*, 97

P

packet boats 38; owned by Rivanna Navigation Company 39
Palmyra 40, 69, 80, 88, 92; 1813 dam 31, 51; 1850 dam 31, *50*, 52–53, 77; 1850 lock *50*, cov-ered bridge 52, *52*, *74*, 75–77; ferry 77; lock stonework *41*,
51; named by Walker Timberlake 51; Pembroke Pettit Bridge 77; stamp based on covered bridge *76*
Palmyra Mills 21, 28, 43, 55, 78–79
Payne, Walter 53
pearlware 94
Pembroke Pettit Bridge 77
Pettit's Island 29
Peyton, Green 67
Pireus *20*, 21, 29, 67, 70; as Port of Albemarle *20*
Point of Fork 6, 14, 16, *17*, 62, *99*
Preddy Creek 4

Q

Quarles, Robert 62
Queen Anne 3, 17

R

Raccoon Creek 7
Randolph, John *27*
Randolph, Thomas Jefferson 27
Randolph, Thomas Mann 12
Rassawek *17*
Richmond and Alleghany Railroad 71, 87, *95*
Richmond 21, 61
Rio Mills 29, 69–70, *91*; covered bridge at 69, *91*; destroyed and rebuilt 30, 69
Rison, John *81*, 85, 88
Rivanna Company 12, 19–21; and Thomas Jefferson 24–25; directors in 1810 19; incorpo-rated 19; tolls 21
Rivanna Connexion Canal 45, *55*, *56*, 57–59, *60*, 81, 87, 88, *89*, *97*; culverts 57; farm road overpass *58*
Rivanna Conservation Society 99, 100
Rivanna Hall 82, *87*
Rivanna Mills 21, 28, 39, 40, 45, 55–57, 64, 80–85, *92*, 93; as Ashlin's Mills *81*, 85; as Rison's Mills *81*, 85; as Stillman's Mills *81*, 85; dam 55, *56*; plat *56*; stonework 83
Rivanna Navigation Company 37, 39, 55, 63, *65*, *66*, 82, 87; assets 63; charter 27; invest-ment 63; presidents of 27; pri-macy of boat navigation rights over mill rights under 28; state investment 27
Rivanna River; and agricultural economy; as North Fork of the James 3, *17*, 68; boat names 64; effect of population
growth 100; effect of power plants 100; effect of reservoirs 100; effect of sewage 14, 100; eras of transportation 1; floods 6, 13, 15, 24, 29, 66; ice 16; in the Revolutionary War 14–15; islands, erosion and reappear-ance 31; locks and dams, inventory of 28; low water *14*, 16, 100; milldams 21; named American Treasure 99; North Fork 4, 19, 21; prospective Buck Mountain reservoir 100; sluice system 27; South Fork 4, 19, 69; South Fork locks and dams 29–31; South Fork reservoir 70; threats to the river 99; Virginia's first Scenic River 99
Rivanna Trails Foundation 99
Rivanna Warehouse 16
Rose, Reverend Robert 12–13, 15
Roundabout Creek 7
Route 15 79
Route 250 bridge *31*
Route 6 59; bridge 29
Route 600 46, 74; bridge *33*
Route 616 *72*, 73
Rucker, Anthony 13
Rucker, Benjamin 13
Runge, Pete 95

S

Sandy Falls 18
Save American Treasures 99
Scenic River Advisory Board 99
Shadwell Dam 67
Shadwell Mills 6, 12, 18, 21, 28, 39, 40, 63, 67, 70–71, 87; burned 71
Shifflett, Linda *95*
slaves 51
Solitude Spring Branch 51
Southwest Mountains 4, 6, 18
steamboat 28, 95; wreckage *95*, 96
Stillman, George 28, *81*, 82, *84*, 87
Stillman, Samuel 82, *84*, 87
Stockton Creek 4
Stockton, Fielding 80
Strange's Farm (*see also* Oak Hill Plantation) 29, 32, 40; batteau lock *33*, 39, *53*, 78
Stump Island 29, 40, 67
Stump Island Dam *61*, 67
Sugar Hollow reservoir 100

T

Tatum, Colonel William 23
Taylor, A.J. 88
Thomas Jefferson Regional Planning District 99
Thompson, George 12
Thompson, Roger 12
Thoreau, Henry David 9
Three Islands 29, 30, 31
Thrift's Ford 40
Timberlake family *35*, *63*, *70*, *72*
Timberlake, John 21, 51, 75, *78*
Timberlake, Walker 21, 27, 50, 53, 75, *78*
towpaths 1, 6; in Virginia 37
Trout, W.E. *31*
Tulloch's Mill 21
Tutwiler, Wesley C. 64

U

Union Hall 72, 73
Union Mills 21, 28, 39–40, 41, 45, 63, 64, 71–73, 80, 88, *92*, 93; dam 44, 45; lock 41, *44*
Union Mills Factory *35*, 71
University of Virginia Department of Landscape Architecture 99

V

Valentine Museum 95
Virginia Air Line Railroad 88
Virginia Board of Public Works 27
Virginia Canals and Navigations Society 1, *31*, *48*, *82*, 94, 99, 100
Virginia Central Railroad 39
Virginia Department of Environmental Quality 100
Virginia Department of Transportation *33*
Virginia Highway Department 77

W

Walker, Dr. Thomas 11, 12
Washington, George 23
water-level bridges *92*, 93
Wertenbaker, T.J. 14
White House Millennium Council 99
White Rock 29, 32, 40, 53; bat-teau lock *33*, 39
White, Wilmer 93
Wildwood Station 63
Wilkerson, Fannie 93
Williamsburg 87
Wills, Fred M. *66*
wing dams 1; construction 19, *21*; in Albemarle County 19–21
Wood's dam 10, 32
Wood's Mill 19, 21, 29, 86
Wood, William 19, 21
Woods, Edgar 66
Woolen Mills, Charlottesville *20*, 70; dam 70, 99

ABOUT THE AUTHORS

MINNIE LEE McGEHEE, a lifelong resident of Fluvanna County, Virginia, has made a continuous study of the Rivanna River for more than 40 years, and first wrote about its history in 1965 for the Charlottesville, Virginia, *Daily Progress*. She has written and researched for the Fluvanna County Historical Society since 1962, having produced 25 full-length manuscripts and edited many others for the Society on a variety of subjects. For 15 years she has contributed articles to publications of the Virginia Canals and Navigations Society, and in 1996 edited a book for the VC&NS, *River Boat Echoes, Batteaux in Virginia*. She appeared before the Virginia General Assembly in 1973 to secure the Rivanna's designation as the first Virginia State Scenic River, and served on the governor's Rivanna Scenic River Advisory Board for 25 years. "My frequent trips along the Rivanna," she writes, "by canoe and on foot, have revealed much of the history and life of the river, and I continue to search for ways to preserve its beauty and its story."

WILLIAM E. TROUT, III, PH.D., of Richmond, a geneticist, has studied canals and navigations throughout the United States, as well as in Canada, England, France and India. He co-founded both the American Canal Society and the Virginia Canals and Navigations Society. In addition to contributing to the publications of both societies, Dr. Trout has completed extensive research and archeological study on the many old navigation systems in Virginia, and has published for the VC&NS 12 atlases with detailed maps and histories, including three on the James River, two on the Appomattox, and atlases for the Shenandoah, the Rivanna and others. At present he is researching the Staunton and New rivers in Virginia.